SHOWING YOUR DOG

If you are the proud owner of a thoroughbred dog, then the chances are that your thoughts will sooner or later—and probably sooner—turn to the possibility of entering your dog at a show. Who knows, he, or she, may well be a potential winner though never aspiring to the exalted rank of champion. Showing a dog is a fascinating and rewarding hobby, and once you have taken the first step you will never look back. How to take that first step, and ensure your dog the best possible chance and yourself the maximum enjoyment, is explained in this book of shrewd advice and practical guidance. The author, the late Leslie Perrins, was one of our foremost authorities on dogs and dog shows.

Frontispiece photograph: The beautiful Yorkshire Terrier Champion Blairsville Royal Seal. During 1976 he was so often at the top a week hardly went by without his photograph being seen in the Dog Press. (Photo: Anne Cumbers)

SHOWING YOUR DOG

LESLIE PERRINS

Revised by

ANNE MACDONALD

FOYLES HANDBOOKS
LONDON

ISBN 0 7071 0614 1

© W. & G. Foyle Ltd. 1964

First published 1964
Reprinted 1967
Reprinted 1970
Revised edition 1980
Reprinted 1985

Published in Great Britain by
W. & G. Foyle Ltd.,
125 Charing Cross Road,
London WC2H 0EB

Line drawings by Leslie Benenson

Photoset in Great Britain by
Photobooks (Bristol) Ltd.

CONTENTS

ILLUSTRATIONS

1

THE KENNEL CLUB

The middle of the nineteenth century found the prosperous and leisured Victorians with a passion for exhibitions and 'instructive entertainments'. The development of the railways brought the whole of the country within reach of the Great Exhibition of 1851, housed in what was to become the Crystal Palace. During the years that followed a series of exhibitions of widely varying character was held.

The first organized dog show was held in the Town Hall, Newcastle-on-Tyne on the 28th and 29th June, 1859. The show was organized by Messrs Shorthose and Pape at the suggestion of Mr R. Brailsford and had sixty entries of Pointers and Setters. There were three judges to each class and one of the judges of Setters succeeded in taking first prize in Pointers, whilst one of the judges of the Pointer classes took first prize in Setters! Only one class was held for each breed at these early shows and the dogs were unidentified except by their kennel names; reference to the old catalogues reveals Mr Murrell's 'Spot' (price £5,000) competing against Mr Brown's 'Venus' (price 22/-). Unfortunately, the name of the winner is not given.

The Calendar gives two shows each year for the next ten years and by this time, 1870, it was obvious that a controlling body was was necessary to legislate in canine matters. The Crystal Palace show was first held in 1870 by the National Dog Club and after the second show Mr S. E. Shirley, Member of Parliament for Ettington, called together that committee and a discussion ensued which resulted in twelve gentlemen meeting at No. 2 Albert Mansions, Victoria Street, London, in April, 1873, and this meeting marked the founding of the Kennel Club. Today, of course, the Kennel Club is the governing body of the world of dogs, just as the Jockey Club is the ruling body in horse racing circles. Mr Shirley was the Kennel Club's first President.

Today the Kennel Club is situated at 1–4 Clarges Street, Piccadilly, London, a delightfully appointed club for a somewhat limited membership, also containing a Ladies' Branch, together with Council Chamber and Committee Rooms. There is large office accommodation for quite a considerable staff, dealing with many thousands of registrations which are made throughout the year, all maintained on a very remarkable filing system. Another department deals with all the business of shows and licensing, another deals exclusively with Crufts, now wholly under the administration of the Kennel Club, which, incidentally, starts preparations for next year's Crufts almost as soon as the lights go down at Olympia on the Crufts of the current year. In fact judges for this world famous show are often selected two and three years ahead of the date. I am always tremendously impressed with the really lovely collection of paintings of dogs and hounds by well known artists hanging on the walls of the various rooms of the Kennel Club, quite superb pictures of which one never tires. When visitors see this impressive club and all it contains for the first time, I think it is realized what an impact the breeding and showing of dogs has made upon this dog loving land of ours.

The Kennel Club was a most necessary institution and through the years it has performed a most useful function and continues to do so. Ordinary dog fanciers like ourselves have every reason to be most grateful to it and to the many people who give of their time to serve on the many committees connected with it.

One of the earliest undertakings of the Kennel Club when it was formed was the compilation of a Stud Book, the editor being Mr Frank C. S. Pearce, the son of the Rev Thomas Pearce, the well known 'Idstone' of *The Field*.

The first volume of the Stud Book contained the records of shows from 1859 and to quote *The History Of The Kennel Club* it was obvious that some system of distinctive nomenclature would have to be introduced to overcome the confusion arising out of 'quantities of Spots, Bobs, Bangs, Jets, Nettles, Vics, most of them insufficiently described and none of them being well-known dogs of the same name'.

In 1880 the Committee introduced a system of 'universal

registration', which was strongly opposed at first, but the advantage of reserving the use of a name for a dog was quickly seen and accepted. Registration in 1880 was nothing more than the registration of a name to avoid duplication in the Stud Book. The pedigree was of little importance and only came as an aid to identification at a later date.

The Committee formulated a code of ten rules relating to dog shows, all of a simple character. It was announced that societies which adopted this code of rules for their shows would be 'recognized' and the winners at their shows would be eligible for the Stud Book. In 1875, the Committee decided to disqualify dogs which were exhibited at unrecognized shows but this rule was not enforced for some years.

The Kennel Gazette was first published in 1880 and has continued as a monthly publication from that date. The Stud Book and Calendar has been published annually, for well over eighty years.

The Committee introduced many rules and regulations and after a few years evolved a system of government which proved so sound that it was adopted as the basis of many overseas kennel clubs. At the end of the century the character of dog showing had so improved that about half of the exhibitors were women, and members of the Royal Family were showing dogs regularly. His Royal Highness the Prince of Wales was a staunch supporter of the movement to prevent the cropping of dogs ears and from 9th April 1898 such dogs have been ineligible for competition.

In 1900 nearly thirty Championship Shows were held and the smaller informal shows were becoming more and more popular. The policy of the Committee was to keep rules and restrictions to a minimum and shows were 'recognized', 'licensed' or 'sanctioned' providing the executive of the show agreed to adopt the Kennel Club show regulations. The guarantors of a show signed an undertaking (and still do) 'to hold and conduct the show under and in accordance with the Rules and Regulations of the Kennel Club'.

The Kennel Club acquired Cruft's Dog Show during the 1939–45 war after the death of Charles Cruft, and has held the Show in February each year at Olympia since 1950. The entry each

successive year has broken all records—in 1960 for example, there were 7,892 dogs of 117 different breeds at the Show and the numbers kept rising until it became necessary for the Kennel Club to introduce some sort of restriction. This was achieved by only allowing dogs which had 'qualified' by winning or being in the first three in certain classes at the championship shows held during the previous year. Even with this 'qualifier' the numbers rose, and there were nearly 9,000 dogs at Olympia for the 1976 Crufts— which resulted in a stiffer qualifier being introduced.

Opposite: Final judging in the arena at Cruft's.

2

TO SHOW OR NOT TO SHOW

Should I show my dog? How often is the experienced dog breeder asked this and how often is the question followed by information such as 'he's very well bred and comes from big kennels. His father was the Champion of England' (a title which does not exist), or 'We think he's very pretty and my neighbour likes him far better than the one she saw at Crufts', and so on and so on.

Well every true dog lover is delighted to know that any dog is appreciated and admired by his owners, but when it comes to entering upon the very fascinating but frequently frustrating business of competing at dog shows, the matter requires a bit of serious consideration.

In the first place, let it be clearly understood that providing your dog is of a pure breed and that he has been registered at the Kennel Club on the Active Register—and always providing his entries have been completed correctly and he is in a state of health and physical condition to pass the requirements of the veterinary surgeons in attendance on the day of the show—any dog can walk into the show ring and take his chance. It is as simple as that.

Is your pet for showing?

At the very beginning of this little book, which, it is hoped, will be of assistance to the absolute beginner in the world of dog showing, with all its strange ways and terms, I would like to offer this piece of advice: If you possess a lovable, friendly dog which was bought as a pet, at a pet price and he fulfils all your requirements as such, please do not ever exhibit him. If on closer acquaintance with his

Opposite: Your lovable family pet may not be suitable for showing— although these prize-winning Whippets are enjoying the warmth and companionship of their young friends.

breed standard and, if on obtaining a little expert advice from a quite impartial source, you come to realize he has many short-comings, this realization may possibly belittle him somewhat in the eyes of the household of which he is a popular and worthy member. Remember, you could easily exchange him for a dog with greater beauty from a show point of view but could you guarantee as nice a disposition? Be grateful for what you have got.

I once sold a Boxer puppy to a man in my profession, telling him that he was buying a youngster quite capable of doing some winning. I was greeted with the reply, 'I wouldn't dream of showing him. My wife and I think he is perfect and I should only feel annoyed if others didn't agree'. Well, it was a point of view and I rather respected it. The dog, incidentally, had a wonderful home and was treasured all his life—to my great satisfaction.

The fact that you or your neighbour may think your dog is very pretty really does not enter into the matter. It may well be that you are not really well versed in the standard devised for the breed and cannot therefore see the faults which would be immediately obvious to an expert. The fact that he is well bred does not, by any means, ensure that his distinguished breeding has produced the desired specimen.

A champion in every litter?

Most breeders would agree that if they could, out of every litter, be sure of producing one puppy with show potentialities, they would be doing quite nicely. Therefore it will be readily appreciated that there are many puppies produced by distinguished parents which are quite typical of their breed, but which are not quite good enough to put into the ring, having faults, slight or otherwise, which would stop them meeting with any real success in com-petitions of any consequence. These same puppies have to be sold to homes in the hands of pet owners, perhaps people who do not desire to pay the price of a puppy up to real show standards and people, maybe, who have no interest in show requirements at all.

From a purely commercial point of view the experienced breeder will want to dispose of the dog puppies falling into the category under discussion. These do not improve in value as the weeks go by and they continue to need food, space and exercise, whereas the well-bred bitch puppy, with certain limitations from a show point of view, may quite well be bought by someone wanting a brood bitch at a lower cost than one capable of winning. Alternatively, she may indeed—in consideration of her pedigree—prove to be worthwhile retaining in the kennel in which she was bred. However, let us assume that the reader has come to the conclusion that he or she would like to embark upon dog showing, and so buys a puppy with that end in view.

So you want to show
First of all, my advice would be for the intending purchaser to visit one or two of the big championship shows held during the year. Having of course decided upon the breed most fancied, study the leading winners and, by so doing, get an overall picture in your mind of the breed you propose to support. I say concentrate upon a championship show, for there will be found the top specimens of the breed you have selected, competing for the most coveted awards, namely, challenge certificates.

Acquire a copy of your breed's standard. This could be described as the blueprint explaining in detail what is required. Standards are drawn up by experts on their breed and have to be approved by the Kennel Club. Standards can be obtained from the Kennel Club. Alternatively practically every breed has a breed club, association or league set up to look after that breed's general interests. If one joins, new members should have no difficulty in obtaining a standard. Some clubs produce handbooks or newsletters, all of which can be instructive to the beginner on joining.

Having done all this our beginner should have absorbed enough knowledge to take the next step and acquire his first dog to be the foundation of his kennel.

3

STARTING OUT

Having definitely decided that you want to show, the next major step will be the purchase of your first show dog.

Buying your first show dog
The man or woman who can say with absolute assurance that any particular puppy will be a certain winner must be, I think, a very remarkable person—so much so, that I am inclined to think that their knowledge in many cases is greatly bolstered up by pure and simple wishful thinking. There is no doubt, however, that some breeders have a very good eye for a puppy. Quite often it will be noticed that these breeders are good with puppies of their own strain and very disappointing over litters of other people's dogs. This is fairly understandable for when one has had several generations of a particular family it is not hard to recognize at once certain family resemblances in puppies, saying to oneself 'that pup is just like old "so and so" when he was that age, he had just that sort of a head' etc. The really experienced breeder however, will usually be wise enough to say 'this puppy with "average luck" should turn out nicely', adding with commendable caution 'as far as one can tell at its present age'. It is the hall-mark of the real amateur to make wide sweeping claims, unless of course the vendor is plainly dishonest. Unfortunately one does not have to travel far to find this sort of person, particularly when coping with transactions over animals, I much regret to say.

So much can go wrong in the course of development, so many swans at three months turn out to be geese when they reach maturity. At the start it must be decided whether a puppy of say ten weeks is to be purchased, with first-class breeding behind it and no apparently glaring faults, which the purchaser can grow on, show and finally breed from. This is quite a usual procedure. It is

A little reassurance

Colour photos by Anne Cumbers

Transporting

On Show

Plenty of water

Training starts early

Judging Pekes

Judging rough collies

Training in ring craft

assumed that in approaching the matter in this way the purchaser will want a bitch.

Secondly a rather older puppy could be bought, one that has already begun its show career and perhaps has already collected a prize card or two. Not so easy to find in the market but not impossible, provided it is understood that a much bigger price will be asked. Then it is sometimes possible to pick up a mature bitch, who has already proved herself a breeder of useful puppies, because she is being offered for sale to make way for younger stock and the owner would like to place her in a good home while she can still produce another litter or so. A reasonable price and a puppy, or perhaps two, is expected in a case like this. Finally, if money is no great problem, then open your cheque book, take proper impartial advice, and buy the best you can. But in this case, no doubt about it, a substantial price will be asked.

Probably the best thing for a beginner is to study the principal exhibitors and, having made your choice, approach that person. Put your cards on the table and ask whether that owner has any stock available, fully explaining the purpose for which the animal is required. If unable to offer anything, it is highly probable that this exhibitor's kennel will contain stud dogs and the owner will know where puppies are available or expected by his stud dogs and will be able to give all sorts of useful advice to the beginner. It is rather a question of finding the right person in the first place. That is half (if not all) the battle. However, use your judgment of the human race which at this stage is probably better than your unaided judgment of dogs. Fortunately there are many more honest people in dogs than dishonest ones, I am indeed happy to say.

Experienced or inexperienced, it is nevertheless possible to be proved very wrong where all classes of animals are concerned. How often can one read of highly successful racehorses passing through the rings at yearling sales with little or no interest on the part of the discerning bloodstock people gathered at the ringside. Equally, some very highly priced and much 'sought after' youngsters just never achieve anything on the racecourse.

With all classes of livestock one is for ever learning and however much one knows, something unusual, something new, will present itself from time to time. So as years roll by, be very cautious when someone starts off by saying to you, 'oh you are an expert', or 'you know all about . . .' You never do!

I have presumed that my reader will start off by purchasing a bitch. Unless wanted purely as a pet, a dog has to achieve a great deal in the show ring before he can be in any sort of demand as a stud dog, and I feel it is unlikely that this highly specialised work would be uppermost in people's minds when taking up show dogs seriously. Do not be persuaded, as some people are, to buy a brace of unrelated puppies with an idea of breeding from these two. It is very unlikely that you would, at the first attempt, secure an outstanding dog and if you are going to the trouble and expense of breeding puppies at all, you must concentrate on tip-top dogs for sires. Given the consideration that the matter demands, it will be found in almost any breed that there are plenty about.

Having acquired your foundation puppy, rear her well and keep her fit. Train her to be handy and fearless of people and the everyday things of life, and sit back and wait, full of excitement I am sure, for that great day when, having turned six months of age, she can set out for her first show. The first, we hope, of many happy and successful shows, the first adjective being quite as important as the other!

Temperament

In some ways, I feel that this is the most important part of my effort to help the beginner. Such a lot is said and written about the subject. I have heard it said that some exhibitors and breeders ruin every breed which they touch. Generally speaking I think this is quite a ridiculous claim. However, just as today one hears far more about nervous breakdowns and the need of psychiatrists for humans, there can be little doubt that nervousness is more apparent in dogs than used to be the case. I am inclined to think this is apparent in all dogs, show dogs, pet dogs, mongrels or purebreeds. Perhaps the noisy world in which we live today has something to do with it.

Nevertheless, I cannot stress too strongly that temperament is something that should be ever present in breeders' minds, and I would be willing to agree that there are some commercially-minded people who pay far too little consideration to this immensely important matter.

The world is full of highly strung, irritable and excitable people and I feel we can have no time for this sort of thing in dogs, who should give their owners pleasure and relaxation. It is not a bit of good producing one dog out of a litter which, with expert handling, can grace the show ring and win prizes and perhaps live his life kennelled, if his brothers and sisters are nervous, over excitable, hard to handle and complete failures in pet homes. They are to be pitied, and so too are their disappointed owners.

It must be agreed, too, that it is the 'bad' dog in a road which is always remembered and how often one hears it said 'Oh! I couldn't have one of that breed, my neighbour had one which was snappy' or 'we had one in our road which was uncertain, a shocking fighter' or something of that sort.

The man in the street can be heard saying that 'In-breeding' is the cause of all this trouble, without having a very clear idea what he is discussing. Close breeding or line breeding can be all right in the experienced hands of people who know their dogs and know what they are aiming to achieve. These people will only practice this in-breeding from stock with a thoroughly sound background, both mental and physical.

Our beginner must therefore do all that is possible to obtain foundation stock bred from parents with good temperaments on both sides. Personally, I take a lot of trouble to get to know any stud dog I may contemplate using. It is not enough for me to be aware of the fact that he has won this and that, and is in popular demand. I like to see him on his bench and if possible in his home, and, by this, I am able to assess what sort of character he has or—as I term it in my own home—what sort of 'person' he is.

Many people in the dog world are inclined to talk and write upon the complicated study of genetics. Unfortunately, I tend to think some of them have only a very limited knowledge of this vast study. I only know from experience that dogs with extremely shy and nervous dispositions are likely to produce progeny with similar disadvantages . Likewise, bad-tempered animals are prone to produce bad-tempered progeny, and the reproduction of this unpleasant trait is something to avoid at all costs.

Further, my own experience also leads me to think that puppies frequently resemble their grandparents rather more than their immediate parents. One of the things that has interested me most in some twenty years of judging has been speculating upon the breeding of a ring full of puppies. As one becomes knowledgeable about a breed over several generations, perhaps, it is fascinating to note the characteristics stamped by certain families.

For myself, I would willingly sacrifice a point or two in beauty in exchange for a bold, happy temperament when planning future breeding.

Finally, my advice to those establishing a kennel: do everything possible to procure foundation stock with good temperaments. Having done this, do all in your power to preserve this quality and by so doing you will be serving well your favourite breed, your future customers and saving yourself endless worries.

Choice of a breed

Now I am well aware that in many cases, people drift into dog showing. A dog is bought primarily as a pet, he turns out rather well and is shown and that's how it all begins, the owner's choice of a breed being fixed from the very beginning. But not always is this the case. There are the people who decide to embark upon dog breeding and showing and have no settled opinions as to the breed to take up. These are the readers who may, I hope, be helped a little by this section, for the matter really requires a good deal of thought. No matter how we approach this curiously fascinating business we are taking on quite a lot of work however pleasurable it may be. Let's face it, some like it 'easy' while others appear to be gluttons for punishment where effort is concerned. There are so many aspects of approach: money, space, time, transport, situation. All these factors must enter into the matter very considerably and each must be given careful consideration if our entry into this recreation is going to be a success and give us the pleasure it should.

At the outset, please let it be understood that this advice is offered with no favouritism and certainly no dislike. I find every breed of dog interesting and only regret it is not possible in life to have personal experience of every one. I do not believe, for one minute, there is such a thing as a 'best breed' and I do not think it is a bit of good anyone taking up a breed which does not really make a personal appeal. This is not the way to succeed. Neither do I think it is a bit of good for a person to run his head into a brick wall and insist on trying to breed a variety of dog with which, from every point of view, he is totally ill-equipped to deal.

In the world of racing one hears the term 'horses for courses' and, I think, in the field we are discussing, one might say 'dogs for people'. Fortunately, I feel tastes vary so very much and it would be dull indeed if our range of choice was more limited. So I repeat my first piece of advice which is that no one should take up a breed which he or she does not care about, whether it be from a point of view just of physical appearance or from the point of view of customary traits of temperament within that breed. By this, I mean that some breeds are by nature fussy and demonstrative while others are inclined to be reserved, somewhat aloof, at any rate as far as strangers are concerned. Some are indoor types and some want wide open spaces and so on. I feel very strongly that it is absolutely essential to like the creatures in one's care, no matter whether they be dogs, horses, cattle or chickens. This surely is the first rule in real animal husbandry. Some time ago, a lady somewhat heavily involved in a certain breed of dog asked me whether she could make her kennels pay if she took up a breed of toy dog although, she added, she couldn't bear little dogs of that sort. Knowing the tremendous individuality of the dogs involved and the great response they give to those who really care for them, I quickly dissuaded the lady. This, quite definitely, is no way to approach dog breeding.

At the same time, if the reader wants to have perhaps several litters a year, then it is necessary for most people to remember that this will mean that there can easily be quite a number of surplus puppies—which may be a problem if a breed is selected for which there is, for some reason, a very limited demand. One can in these circumstances so soon find the production lines choked, which is both disappointing and difficult.

Certain breeds need so much more exercise than others. Are you able to supply them with adequate exercise in the way of a fenced-in paddock or have you time to do a good deal of road walking? No dogs can be expected to succeed in the show ring if never given sufficient exercise and in this respect I am sure that many kennel establishments are at fault.

To continue with the problems of selecting a breed. Where do you live? If the reply to this question is a suburban district or a built-up area then it is very advisable to give serious consideration to dogs that do not bark too much. There are breeds which, though they may have many attractions, are disposed to give tongue very readily; too readily, perhaps, for a slightly irritable non-dog-loving neighbour, and difficulties of this sort can be so tedious and tiresome.

In my experience dogs that are primarily herding dogs tend to have this inclination when kennelled or kept in numbers, whereas dogs of the Bull breeds (Bulldogs, Boxers, French Bulldogs, etc.) seem to be more manageable in this respect. On this matter I must say that general management, in accordance with the particular requirements of the owner, can greatly influence this matter of noise—insufficient exercise or time out of their kennels, irregularities in feeding, inadequate feeding, draughty kennels and uncomfortable bedding. All these things add up to creating noisy dogs which give cause for complaints and unpleasantness. At one time a woman friend went in for a certain type of foreign hound, and most decorative the animals were, but unhappily they would arise with the dawn and howl. This, needless to say, was entirely unappreciated by her neighbours in the built-up area in which she lived and inevitably the hounds had to go. I would not, for one minute, claim that this predisposition was typical of the breed in question—it may possibly have been some fault in management—but it was a most regrettable end to something that started with such promise.

The big breeds.   You may have a great yearning to keep dogs of great size and this matter can be viewed from two angles at the very outset. There are the big solidly-built breeds such as St Bernards, Mastiffs, Newfoundland, Great Danes and Irish Wolfhounds. Then there are the big breeds—or perhaps one should say the 'tall' breeds—which are of much lighter build such as Borzois, Deer-

Opposite: How bigger can you get? A benched St Bernard with owner.

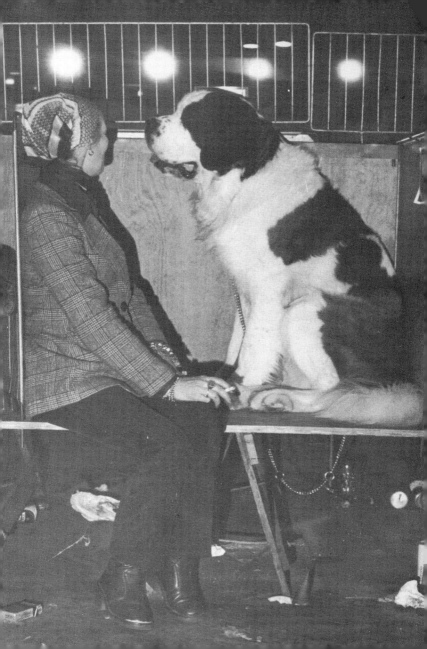

hounds and Greyhounds (or Longtails as the professional dog man is in the habit of calling them), Salukis and Afghans. Of this lovely section of the dog world, I would venture to suggest that the first group contains some of our most impressive dogs but it must be remembered that it is not everybody who is prepared to give them the amount of food these giants require, nor has everybody the space they need to be happy and comfortable. They mostly require good solid walking for exercise rather than fast gallops and sharp bursts of speed. These factors, it has to be admitted, present the average pet owner with problems with which they cannot very easily cope and the sad result is a rather limited market. Also, big breeds have what I think they describe in pig breeding as a high fecundity average; in other words, they do have biggish litters.

It could be quite a problem, as an unknown breeder, to find oneself with perhaps seven or eight fast growing puppies and no prospective purchasers. A responsibility too, for these large dogs must be reared well and any lover of animals will agree that they must go into the hands of people ready to give them what they need. In my opinion it is quite amoral to shirk this responsibility. I feel, as I write these lines, that I am, perhaps, appearing to discourage lovers of big dogs. This is far from my intention. I like these lovely breeds so much that I think it is only fair to them to ensure their well-being.

What then of the many breeds which may still be classed as big breeds, but less massive or less tall than the ones already listed?

Into this section come many gun dogs: Setters, Pointers, Retrievers, including Labradors, Goldens, Curly coated, flat coats and the lesser known Chesapeake Bay. Then that wonderful dog, the Alsatian or German Shepherd, which, given the right strain and an understanding owner, is a quite outstanding dog in any company. The not very well-known Rottweiller, the Rhodesian Ridgeback, the Old English Sheepdog, the Doberman, the Bull Mastiff, Collies both smooth and rough and their relatives the Bearded Collies, the noble and unusual looking Bloodhound. Continuing to move down a little in the matter of size we still remain with the big dogs and find two more gun dogs, the German Short-haired Pointer, the Polish shooting dog, the Wiemaraner, unusually of a silvery-grey colour with merle or blue eyes. That popular, boisterous and usually sweet-natured dog the Boxer bring this quick survey down to dogs of about 24–25 inches (60–63 cm) at the shoulder, and the smart carriage dog of days gone by, the Dalmatian.

Whereas all the breeds we have mentioned could, I expect, be kept in all sorts of homes by people just wanting one dog as a pet, when it comes to breeding and rearing litters of puppies the viewpoint must change considerably. They are all capable of taking a lot of exercise and indeed many of them are hounds or shooting dogs which were originally required and bred to work. They require roomy kennels and runs and since the puppies are mostly heavy, they do not want serious walking. Rather do they require large sunny runs and a paddock in which to play. Although very active and strong these big puppies, like small children, soon get tired. However, when puppyhood has gone, exercise and plenty of it they must have. Can this be organized for them? The odd quarter of an hour on fine days before the rush for the business train just will not do. Of course if help in the family is forthcoming or if labour is available in the shape of kennelmaids the whole vista is changed.

One final thing before leaving the 'big uns'. If showing is to be seriously undertaken a roomy means of transport, in the way of a van or estate car, can be considered an essential. Very big dogs, however good and handy they may be, present problems on railways, and insurmountable ones if the owner has several dogs entered for a distant show. I once knew a lady who at a time of terrific enthusiasm would take three large hounds from the South of England to Glasgow or Edinburgh shows, travelling overnight in the Guard's Van, sitting on rugs with the hounds. She deserved all the cups she could win but she's not in dogs now!

Before passing on let it be said that if the requirements—financial, space and food—of these big dogs can be supplied, my reader will be able to make a selection from some of our loveliest representatives in the world of dogs, the owning of which should give both pride and pleasure, but, in fairness to the dogs themselves, be fully prepared to provide them with what they require. There is no cheap, cheese-paring way to get round this matter.

Terriers. And so we come to smaller dogs altogether, using as a sort of link the Airedale which introduces us to the great family of terriers. Now a great many people are very attracted to terriers of various kinds and, indeed, this is very understandable. However, one must appreciate that a lot of them want a good deal of very skilful preparation to present them in the ring with any real hopes of success. Particularly am I thinking of Airedales, Wire-Haired Fox Terriers, Irish Terriers, Lakelands, Welsh Terriers, Scottish Terriers and West Highlands. Just take a look at a class of these dogs at a championship show and then think of the more humble specimens you can see in the streets. In many cases one would hardly recognize them as of the same breed. I suppose in this section are to be found more professional handlers, highly experienced in stripping and trimming, than in any other. If you are a beginner and you are lucky enough to be possessed of a really good dog, please don't think you can read an article or two on 'how to do it' and then set about your dog. The odds are that you will probably ruin your dogs appearance from a ring point of view for months to come. Go and learn from a real craftsman and maybe, if you keep at it, in about a couple of years you may begin to be quite good and when you have acquired the ability there's a lot of personal satisfaction to be got out of it.

Another terrier needing a deal of show presentation is the Kerry Blue. Less work is needed by the wise-looking Cairn, the Australian, and the Norwich, both prick and drop eared, a delightful little terrier which seems to be deservedly moving up the popularity poll. Then we have the Dandy Dinmont and the Skye, quite a picture when immaculately presented which they really must be. The Beddlington is rather simpler in preparation though still demanding if he's to look his best. Naturally the smooth Fox Terrier demands very little work by comparison, and the same can be said of the Manchester (or Black and Tan) as the man in the street is inclined to call them.

The Bull Terrier is a grand breed with generally most likeable disposition. Coloured ones are easy but if showing whites you will have to don an overall at the shows and join the 'Chalking'

Opposite: A Spitz Samoyed in full winter coat and waiting to be judged.

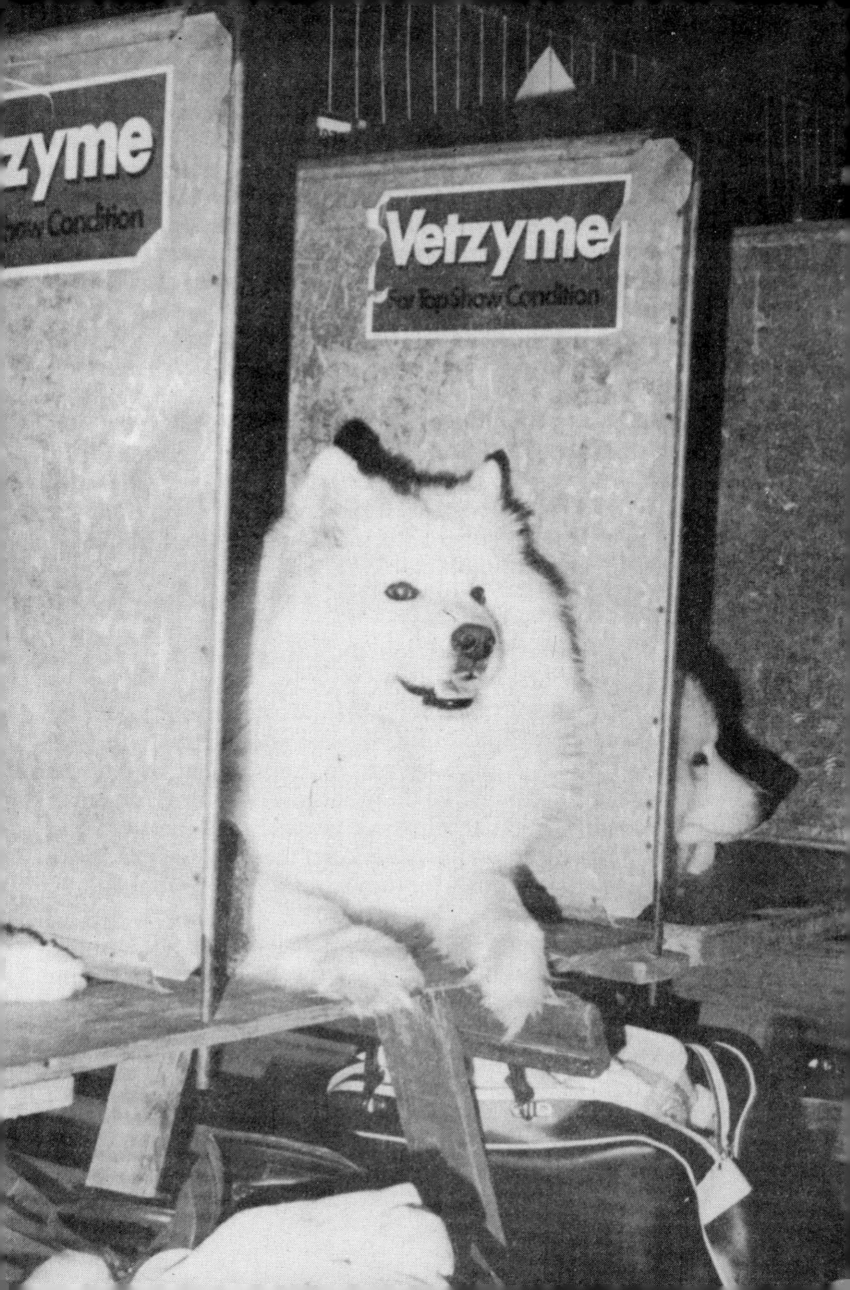
Vetzyme
For Top Show Condition

brigade. Smaller and much more commonplace looking, the Staffordshire is a breed which grows upon one, I find. Their temperaments can be quite delightful with people. Just keep these breeds from becoming confirmed fighters, for, after all, this comes very easily to them.

A very smart, small Boston always captures the eye at a show. They are easy in preparation though often not the best of whelpers from the point of view of breeders.

Spaniels.   So much for the terrier group. Do you care for the spaniels? Many people do and this attraction is very easy to understand, I feel.

No introduction to the Cocker is needed, a beautiful breed, but here you must expect very keen competition and quite a bit of preparation if you want to stand a chance. This applies especially in America. What about the Springer, a handsome bigger Spaniel, or the rather rare Field Spaniel with his great length of body? Or the comfortable and amiable looking Sussex with his liver-coloured coat, and the Welsh Springer, a nice variety with his unusual, rather unspaniel-like, ears.

Before leaving this section we must not forget the Irish Water Spaniel which is not often seen these days.

Spitz.   The spitz group of dogs which attract a lot of people, includes the Norwegian Elkhound, the Keeshond, the Samoyed and the Finnish Spitz. A pleasing group, and bigger, of course, than the terriers and spaniels. To do well these dogs must demand plenty of grooming to get the lustre that their full heavy coats require, and one must be prepared to keep them out of the show ring when they are 'out of coat' for they cannot then do themselves credit.

This section is capable of taking a good deal of exercise and the dogs seem to revel in hard weather. Perhaps the handsome Chow with his oriental look will capture your vote. It is a handsome breed when presented in full coat and produces some of the loveliest looking puppies in dogdom.

Hounds.   Here, perhaps, we should think of two hounds: firstly the quaint, unusual looking Bassett Hound, a breed which seems to have gained quite a lot of ground during the last few years. In spite of the fact that a Bassett is not tall, he is surprisingly weighty and long. Mostly of amiable, placid, indeed rather phlegmatic disposition, he is quite capable of plodding his way for quite long walks. Here too there is a puppy of great appeal, solemn and judicial. A friend introduced one to her home and was shocked a few days later to hear her crying bitterly in the garden. On rushing out to discover the cause she found the Bassett standing on one of her own ears, apparently unable to fathom why she was anchored to the spot or why she had a pain in it. A rather charming story, I thought. Appreciably smaller, the Beagles' popularity has also increased.

4

BEFORE THE SHOW

Before you attend your first show there are a few things you must see to.

Entering your dog
In the first place, your dog must have already been registered at the Kennel Club on the Registration of a Litter register, and possibly on the Basic Register, when it received its Kennel Club name. Now it will be necessary to have your dog put on the Active Register (unless it was born before 31st March 1976 and was registered under the old single-tier system). Any dog which is to be shown, bred from, or exported, must be on the Active Register and since the Kennel Club is always inundated with work, this should be done as soon as you decide you would like to enter the show ring, and not just a few weeks before the show date. The entries for any show usually close at least four weeks before the date of the show, and your registration number will have to be noted on the entry form, so it will be necessary to have your dog placed on the Active Register at least two months before the show.

As a budding exhibitor it would be wise to become a regular subscriber to one of the two dog papers which are published every Friday and contain advertisements of all the forthcoming shows, giving the various breeds to be classified and the judges' names, together with the secretary's name, address and telephone number. Notice of the closing date for entries will also be given. Having selected a suitable show, write or phone the secretary and ask for a schedule, which is to all intents and purposes a list of the various classes allotted to each breed, and contains certain Kennel Club rulings governing the entering of exhibits, details of special prizes to be won, times of judging, closing of show and, sometimes in the case of big shows a map showing the precise situation of the hall or ground where the show is to be held. This can be a great assistance to exhibitors and judges too when making a long journey to a completely strange place.

If this is the very beginning for exhibitor and dog, I would suggest that a smallish show, and one not very distant, might be the wisest choice. It must be remembered that to start off with a big championship show is rather like putting a horse which has never seen a racecourse into one of the Classics, ridden by an apprentice who has never ridden in public before. A small show will be found much less confusing and will provide a little experience for owner and dog. Further, a long train journey or car ride can completely upset a puppy which has, hitherto, scarcely left its own door-step. So 'start small' as they say and hope for bigger things to come.

So the show is selected and the schedule is in front of you. New to all this, the aspiring owner can find all the jargon of classification a real puzzle. Really it is pretty simple, for it is no more than a sort of handicap, making it reasonably possible for everyone to have a fair crack of the whip. Obviously it would be unfair for a champion of mature age to enter a puppy class or a class containing only dogs which have never won a first prize to the value of a pound at any show. Mind you, looking at the position in reverse, if an owner thinks he possesses a superlative puppy making its first appearance in public it is possible for this puppy to be 'put through his classes' which means that, as he progresses through the classsification he is taking on dogs with more and more achievements to their credit until he finally reaches the open class which will be his stiffest test. In reference 'he' and 'his classes', it is perhaps unnecessary to state that the same ruling applies to bitches as it does to dogs.

Sometimes the wonder youngster will succeed. I have on one or two occasions given challenge certificates and best of breed awards to entries still eligible for puppy classes. Some judges are disinclined to give the top award to a dog under twelve months of age and consider it a very bold step to take; indeed, there is always a chance that one so young may not mature quite as well as it promises. However, I feel that an unbeaten puppy has the right to challenge for the top award. A judge, after all, is asked to judge what is before him 'on the day' and not speculate into the future.

Following this section will be found complete details of the different types of shows which are permitted by the Kennel Club and a complete description of the classifications which are allowed at these different events. It is interesting to try and memorize these details. If you can, you will have achieved something that exhibitors of long experience seldom seem able to do with any considerable degree of accuracy.

Carefully note the closing date for the show and as long as the postmark on the envelope containing your entries carries this date on the stamping, your entry will be acceptable.

On the form itself you will be required to give first, the dog's name, under which it is registered and transferred to your ownership, then its breed and sex followed by the registered names of sire and dam. If the dog is for sale the price asked and lastly the numbers of the classes it is desired to enter. These details should be put in block letters in the appropriate places.

On every entry form will be found a declaration to be signed by the exhibitor to the effect that the dog being entered has not been in contact with contagious diseases within the specified time stated, and, of course, the name and address of the owner has to be given in the space designed for this purpose.

Big shows make a practice of supplying benching space for each dog. This is a very costly business. At the time of writing there are only two firms who contract this work, which demands a good deal of labour since all these portable benches have to have the necessary transport and staff to erect them, either on the morning of the show or, at our biggest shows, the day before, and then have to be dismantled again afterwards. The cost is customarily carried by the exhibitors, the usual cost being at present time about 45p per dog, payable at the time of making the entry. However, at the smaller shows, one frequently finds that the shows are described as unbenched, which means just what it states and owners have to take entire charge of their dogs, very often making good use of their estate cars or vans if more than one dog is being exhibited by the same owner, always providing of course, that there is parking

Opposite: A happily benched Bulldog.

space on the ground where the show is taking place, or outside the Hall when the event is an indoor one.

Be sure to post the entry form in good time and remember to enclose your cheque or postal order. In due course, a few days before the show, you will receive an exhibitors' ticket stating your dogs' show number. You are now all set to start the 'dog game'.

Show classifications

Before a show can be held, an application for a licence has to be sent to the Kennel Club. Provided this is granted, in due course a schedule of the proposed classes and the breeds for which they have been selected also has to be submitted. Now, there are different sets of classes allowed for different shows.

Puppy.   This is confined to animals of six months (no dog can be shown under this age) and not over twelve months, at which age it is not considered to be a puppy. At some shows this class can contain dog and bitch puppies; at other shows each sex has a separate class to itself. This is one of the most interesting classes to judge, for in it one can sometimes see future champions and it is always fascinating to follow the careers of these babies. At most championship shows, there is a special puppy class and this is restricted to puppies of between six and nine months.

Junior.   In this class can be entered animals of six but not exceeding eighteen months on the day of the show or, in the case of a two day event, on the first day of the show. A rather adventurous one for the exhibitor for it is possible to find a young dog here of say seventeen and a half months which has already done a lot of winning at an early age. In fact, from a judge's point of view, the eventual best of breed could be here.

Maiden.   In this can be entered dogs which have never won a challenge certificate and which have never been awarded a *first prize* at an open or championship show (puppy and special puppy classes do not count). A useful one this for the dog which has, as yet, only met with very modest success if any.

Novice.   This class is only for dogs which have not won more than three first prizes at an open or championship show (not counting puppy or special puppy classes).

Tyro.   You will not be able to enter your dog in this class if he has won five or more first prizes at an open or championship show (again puppy and special puppy classes not counting).

Debutant. A nice class for beginners. Only open to exhibits which have not won a first prize at a championship show (not counting puppy or special puppy).

Undergraduate. If your dog has won three or more first prizes at championship shows (puppy and special puppy not counting), this class cannot be entered.

Graduate. For dogs which have not won four or more first prizes at championship shows in graduate, post-graduate, minor limit, mid-limit, limit and open classes.

Post-Graduate. Restricted to dogs which have not won five or more first prizes at championship shows in post-graduate, minor limit, mid-limit, limit and open classes.

No dog which has been awarded a challenge certificate can enter any of the foregoing classes, unless they are restricted simply by age, i.e. puppy, junior, special yearling (which is for dogs up to the age of two years on the first day of the show). If your dog has been one of the lucky ones and received this honour, it is only eligible for entry into one of the following classes.

Minor limit. For dogs which have not won two challenge certificates or three or more first prizes at championship shows in minor limit or higher classes at shows where challenge certificates were offered for the breed.

Mid-limit. For dogs which have not won three challenge certificates or five or more first prizes in mid-limit or above, where challenge certificates were on offer for the breed.

Limit. For dogs which have not won three challenge certificates under three different judges or seven first prizes in all in limit and open classes where challenge certificates were on offer for the breed.

Open. As is implied, this is open to all dogs, but if confined to a breed is quite naturally only available for dogs of the breed specified.

Veteran. Subject to the age limit specified but must be for dogs older than five years and, if confined to breed, is only open to that breed.

Field trial. Designed for winners of prizes, diplomas etc. in actual recognized field trial competition.

Brace. You can enter two exhibits here and they can be of the same sex or one of each sex. But you have to be the owner of both dogs and you will have had to enter each animal in some other class or classes at the show.

Preparing for the show

Take a look at any 'best in show' class at a reasonably big open show, and there we can find a wonderful assortment of dogs, each of which will that day have won the coveted award of best of his breed, consequently qualifying to challenge for best of all breeds or best in show. We see dogs of all sizes, of all shapes and, to me, it is amazing to think that through the ages they have all been developed in many parts of the world from a common root stock. We can see the little Chihuahua standing next to the Irish Wolfhound. How, one wonders, has it all happened, so widely different are they. We see sleek short coats such as Whippets, smooth Dachshunds and Boxers possess, dogs with a smooth silky appearance and fringed coat like the Saluki. Others with profuse coats such as the rough Collie, the old English Bobtail and the Keeshond, the Peke with his gorgeous plume so carefully spread out over his back, the little Yorkie standing on his basket, his coat parted down the middle and hanging down on each side of him like a cape and his carefully tended 'falls'. Next look at the many Wirehaired Terriers, lovingly stripped, with their pronounced eyebrows and carefully prepared muzzles giving that 'beard' effect. The Afghan in all his wealth of coat and trousered appearance, not forgetting his very individual top knot of course. All these and many more, down to one of the world's most popular dogs, the Poodle, skilfully presented in all the glory of his lion clip.

Now in a book such as this, it would be quite impossible to give details of how to put each breed 'down', as we commonly term it, for exhibition, nor would I believe any one person could claim to have expert knowledge in every direction although many skilled judges are very well aware of what the finished effect should be like.

Quite a lot of breeds are very simple. The Whippet and the

Opposite: One of the 'simpler' breeds as far as preparation is concerned—a Whippet being groomed with a hound glove.

Boxer, for example, depend on simply condition, cleanliness, regular grooming with a hound glove or the bare hand itself, and general good health.

In considering the wirehaired group, such as Wirehaired Fox Terriers, Scotties, Lakelands, Airedales etc., I am absolutely certain that these breeds require a great deal of skill if they are to be presented correctly, and the best advice I can offer is that the aspiring exhibitor should contact a well-known breeder or professional handler and ask him (or her) to prepare the youngster for his first appearance and give you a lesson at the same time. By all means, if you have acquired a book on your particular breed, study anything it may have to say, but I really think one practical demonstration will be by far the best approach.

Of course, the same applies to the poodle which in all probability requires more expert attention than any other breed, and indeed few dogs are more rewarding. But practical knowledge you must obtain, and then a lot of practice will be necessary before you even begin to be good at the job. Once, when sharing the 'best in show' judging with another judge, I gave the top award to a magnificently presented Miniature Poodle called Blaskeens Oscar of the Waldorf. His immaculate presentation so impressed me that I asked his kennelmaid handler how long she had been working on the dog the day before and she replied, 'oh, about five hours'.

So you will gather that there is no quick way round this job, and you must realize that with so many expert people about, it is a waste of time and one's money to enter a decent dog unskilfully presented. There are so many little tips only known to the old hands in their own particular breed, and many of these fanciers would have little or no idea about how to prepare some other type of dog, having concentrated for so long on one breed. In fact it is quite surprising to find how mono-minded many people are about dogs. Not long ago a lady said to me, 'as far as I am concerned there are just Corgis and other dogs', and that sums up many people in this dog show game.

However, to return to preparation. If you decide to take up a dog with a coat that requires rather a lot of practice and experience and you decide, as I have advised, to benefit at first from practical assistance and advice, do make sure that you are putting yourself and, what is more important, the dog, in the right hands or it will be a question of the blind leading the blind. There are many people who profess to be able to strip terriers and trim poodles, and advertisements appear all over the place to this effect, but I am not at all convinced that many of them are really very expert. Remember, you require this work for the 'show' ring and not just to make a pet look reasonably presentable, which can be quite a different thing. With the greatest respect I suggest that you should not expect this very specialised work to be part of your veterinary surgeon's job. His great knowledge is required to keep the dog in health, not to groom him for showing. I constantly see terriers and poodles which have been put in the hands of poorly qualified people and the results in many cases are appalling.

Take the best Poodle in the world and see what a complete mess an amateur can make of him and you'll appreciate what I am trying to explain. Believe you me, it could take months to make the dog presentable again.

Forgetting these more difficult problems, however, and returning to the more straightforward breeds, your first essential in the ring is complete fitness, and this can only be achieved by a sufficiency of exercise and the right food. Any breed must be in hard condition, well covered, definitely not fat but not lean and scraggy looking. Dogs are like people. Looking their best, certain individual specimens will appear better carrying rather more weight than others. Only your personal knowledge of your own dogs will tell you this with experience. The coat of any dog should shine with fitness, and experience has taught me that this is only an indication of inside health. In my opinion the feeding of the occasional raw egg is a wonderfully beneficial coat conditioner. This plus a clean exterior, regular brushing or grooming with a hound glove, finishing off with the bare hand will be all that the easy-coated breeds require.

A day or so before a show, a good bath followed by careful rinsing and drying should produce a dog that any judge can handle without soiling his hands. This I might say, as a judge, is something quite easily overlooked and one frequently finds one's hands absolutely dirty after handling just a few exhibits. I suggest bathing a day or so before the show as this enables the coat to get back its normal lustre. Some coats, such as a Corgi's, tend to fluff up over much immediately after bathing. Collie people are rather chary of this as bathing tends to make a coat somewhat 'wavey', which is not desired.

Given at the right time, however, bathing smartens up a dog very considerably, especially where the coat carries a lot of white, and all the 'chalking' (permissible in some breeds) fails in its objective if the base is grubby. It's the same if you try to paint over an unprepared base or, I believe, if a woman tries to put make-up on top of an uncleansed face!

See that the dog's face and eyes are clean and dry and avoid stained eye channel. The occasional bathing of the eyes with boracic lotion followed by careful drying should accomplish this. Next we come to feet, a really important feature in any breed and one frequently receiving too little attention. There is little doubt that road walking is almost unbeatable in tightening the feet and keeping nails in trim. But the fact remains that an increasing number of roads are unsuitable for dogs today. Apart from traffic dangers more and more places are imposing regulations about the soiling of pavements, which is quite understandable. But we have to admit that many dogs are exercised in paddocks, woods, on commons, parks and other open spaces which are usually grassland. The foot, therefore, does not get the hard surface exercise necessary to keep the nails worn down, and long nails can cause a foot to misshapen and splayed and spoil a dog's action. More and more dogs have to have their nails cut, therefore there are several excellent clippers on the market, but please seek a skilled demonstration before trying to use them yourself. On no account must the nail be cut down to the quick. This will cause considerable pain to the dog. He may never forget the experience and will be awkward for the rest of his days when nail clipping sessions come round.

Leaving for the show
There is not much advice that can be given here, for all that is really required is commonsense.

Opposite: Suitable road walking is unbeatable for keeping the nails in trim.

Make sure of your route to this, your first show, whether your journey is to be made by car or public transport, and allow plenty of time for the journey. There are few things more frustrating than having to hurry and arrive in a flustered, exhausted condition. It will spoil your day and may well spoil your dog's chances too. A dog is, I think, very conscious of nervous agitation and irritability on the part of his owner or handler. So get off to a calm start and, what is quite as important, try to stay that way all of the day.

I would most strongly urge that, whatever time you have to start, you give your dog ten minutes or so to stretch his legs and relieve himself. I know it can be an effort and I am only too well aware that it can mean sponging a dog's legs and feet and towelling his underparts . . . just one more job when you are in a rush. However, dogs are very conscious of any routine change and some will positively refuse to attend to the laws of nature at all, and some will wait until they get into the ring which can be a nuisance to everyone. If these matters can be achieved on the 'home ground' so to speak, it's well worth the trouble taken and the owner will be spared anxieties and possible accidents in tube and bus and train, let alone the car or van. Too many people are careless in this respect and these are the people who get dogs a bad name and cause the car parks and approaches to shows to become unpleasant and an eye sore to the general public.

Provide for your needs at the show. The rug or blanket for the bench, benching chain and reliable collar which cannot be slipped, the show lead, whatever you may require in the way of grooming materials, which must, of course depend on your breed. Some food for the dog, a small dish for water on his bench and don't forget a little bait to encourage him to give his best in the ring . . . a little well-cooked liver perhaps, cut up into small pieces. Don't overdo this, by the way. I seem to remember a lady who entered the ring with seemingly 'everything but the kitchen stove', large pieces of meat, bones to be followed by bouncing balls, little toys that squeaked—all being offered to the exhibit in a spirit of frenzied excitement. I also seem to remember quite an astonishing lack of

Opposite: Provide for your needs at the show—including the good old thermos flask!

response from the dog! One doesn't see the professional handler acting in this way. However, there is no doubt that the occasional tit-bit and the knowledge that there is more in the hand will tend to stop interest flagging and keep the pride of your kennel awake and on his toes.

Finally, your good self requires a bit of consideration. I hope that aspirin, indigestion tablets and sal volatile will not be needed, but I do suggest that the good old thermos flask should go along with you and possibly a sandwich or two. Generally speaking, catering at shows is pretty rough-and-ready, apart from alcoholic assistance which, of course, can drown disappointments and help to celebrate victories, whichever may come your way. When one gets to the really top shows at places like Olympia, there is ample choice in the way of luncheons and snacks, but some people find it an economy to take something along, for, let's face it, meals are not cheap as a rule. Other people find they would rather stay near their dogs and here again the sandwich and the thermos help to fill the gaping void, for if you are like me you'll find that one gets an appetite standing about all day. Finally, before you shut the front door see that you have the entrance ticket for yourself and dog.

Perhaps as you set off I might wish you good luck.

5

THE SHOW

There are four things to consider when attending a show: your arrival, the organization of the show, time in the ring, and your departure.

On arrival
Now at most shows judging begins around 10.30 a.m. At the beginning of schedules it will be found that dogs are received at the site of the show from, say, nine o'clock onwards, but there will be a final time limit set after which no exhibits will be allowed to enter except under very exceptional circumstances. It will be necessary, therefore, to time one's arrival to fit in with these rulings.

Now let us suppose the show is a championship one and our breed a popular one. A glance at the classification will show you that there will be anything from four to seven classes devoted to each sex and it is the customary procedure for all the 'dog' (as distinct from 'bitch') classes, right down to open dog, to be judged first. If, therefore, we are only showing a bitch, we can probably take advantage of the late arrival ruling which may well be of considerable help since, naturally this means a later start—advantageous for those of us who live in 'do it yourself' homes and if the show is quite a distance away.

Of course, if the time factor is of no great consequence it is very well worthwhile trying to see as much as is possible, for that is the way to learn. All the time one is acquainting oneself with judges' methods and seeing different dogs and different styles of handling. In any case, plan to reach the show with time in hand. A hurried, flustered arrival will reflect upon the dog especially if he is a youngster, unused to all the noise and bustle.

At the show

We are now at the show and this may be a benched or an unbenched one. If we are at a championship show or, in fact, a show of any size, it will undoubtedly be benched, which means that each exhibitor will have paid a fee of probably 45p (costs are rising all the time) in order that his exhibit or exhibits shall be each provided with a compartment, varying in size, of course, according to the breed, where the dog must be chained to either or both of the two rings which are attached to the back of the section. On the back of each bench at about eye level height will be found the number of the dog entered corresponding with the particular dog's number in the catalogue and on the ticket of admittance supplied to the exhibitor.

At an 'out of doors' summer show, these benches will be erected in a series of marquees or large tents and it will be found that quite frequently big breeds will be benched together and so will terriers, gun dogs, non-sporting breeds and toys. In the case of the toy breeds, it will be found that they will be provided with a cage, rather than a bench and these cages are often arranged in two tiers. They are approximately the size of a largish parrot cage. Dogs placed in these cages, needless to say, do not require to be chained, though many people take the added precaution of carrying a small padlock for the wire door.

The first thing, then, on arrival is to find our section and ultimately our bench. Having located it, there are one or two points to bear in mind. Firstly, the bench allotted to our exhibit will be devoid of any form of bedding. Neither will the exhibitor be allowed to bed down the dog on any hay, straw, wood, wool, fibre or anything of this nature for very obvious reasons. It will be agreed that this is only a very sound precaution against fire which is in every person's interest. It is advisable, therefore, to arrive with some sort of comfort and warmth for the dog in the shape of a rug or blanket. Some exhibitors are very ingenious about this sort of

Opposite: Arriving at the Show at the start of a long day which may end in disappointment, satisfaction or delight. Whichever way it ends, the beginning is the same for all: early rising, bags and baggage, journeys, preparation of dogs—and hope! (Photo: Anne Cumbers)

thing and are given to using the same coloured floor covering for all their dogs, which makes the whole thing look more colourful and less prison-like.

Don't forget the regulations require that an exhibit is chained to the rings on the bench. This ruling is often not respected nearly as much as it should be, and the dogs can be seen tied up with light show leads or quite thin exercise leads. I feel this is a rather risky procedure on the part of the owner. How easily can an excited or nervous puppy or young dog, disliking the noise and commotion and finding its owner is not in sight, bite through its lead and escape from its bench and run wild, getting more and more agitated as various people pursue it. Pandemonium can exist and all sorts of disaster can follow in its wake. So buy a proper bench chain and use it—a not too heavy one if the breed is a small one— and see that the dog's collar will not allow the dog to slip his head out of it. Further do not leave the dog sufficient length of chain that will allow him to get off the bench. I have seen dogs so carelessly chained that the dog can get partly off the bench and nearly hang himself.

In the case of toy breeds requiring no chaining in their little show pens, some owners are very full of ideas and the cages are very nicely set out, often having three sides of the pen facing the visitors, covered in gaily-coloured material and a cushion for the dog got up in the same materials or colour. It all helps to make the whole thing more colourful. At a recent show devoted to a particular toy breed, the executive had notices for display reading 'hugs and squeezes spread diseases', which is perfectly true and not a bad idea, I felt. When you have experienced the tiring effect of a non-benched show, where one has to have the dog or dogs on leads all day, or with toy dogs in their baskets, I think one can safely expect you to feel that the benching fee is well worth the money and the price not at all excessive!

So we have at last got our dog on his bench and given him the chance to settle down a bit, perhaps offering him a drop of milk or

Opposite: Final preparations at a large summer championship show. The Airedale is a 'trimmed' dog and there always seems to be 'just that little bit more' which needs tidying. (Photo: Anne Cumbers)

a drink of water and a tit-bit. It's a good thing I consider to try, at all times, to make the dog associate his show bench with a few pleasurable things. He is much more likely to settle down quickly and be contented. Next it is a good idea to possess yourself of a catalogue if, indeed, you have not already done this on arrival, for they are usually on sale at the entrance. Catalogues always seem such a lot of money, but when you have served on a committee running a show you will realize what an enormous amount they cost to get produced, and printing costs seem to keep mounting up.

Now it is worthwhile finding out which of the many rings is allotted to our breed, locate it and if a steward, who will be wearing a badge, appears to be not too harassed, politely enquire from him when your first class is likely to be required in the ring. This done and another glance at our dog to see that he is settling down and appears calm and unruffled, the budding exhibitor might then consult the catalogue and with its help spend a little time having a look at other exhibits and possible rivals on neighbouring benches.

It is never advisable to leave a novice dog for long or drift away too far. The new experience, the general atmosphere added to the barking of other agitated or excited dogs, tends to make life pretty trying until he becomes a hardened campaigner, by which time he will in all probability jump up on his bench, take a rather bored look at the overall picture, promptly turn his back on the whole proceedings and go to sleep. The only problem left by then will be to try and arouse him to some degree of interest! When the time comes to leave the show and start the trek home, he may look full of fire and never so elegant, and you will be thinking 'If only he'd looked like that in the ring!' That is the show game all over.

In the ring

The time gets near and it would be a good idea, perhaps, to get our dog off his bench, straighten him up a bit in the matter of appearance (this procedure must, of necessity, vary with the breed), and let him have a little exercise (on the lead, of course), which will allow him to attend to the needs of nature, which is much more desirable than in the ring itself. At open air shows there are usually lots of places to take dogs and, quite naturally it is advisable to try and find some not too frequented spot nearby. At big indoor shows, certain rings, amply provided with sawdust are always available and sometimes there are yards outside the actual building itself but still within the confines of the show.

It must be remembered that no dogs can be removed from the area enclosed for the show until its removal card can be produced at the show's official closing time, or with a special early removal pass which can be obtained from the show secretary, application for which should be made at the time of sending off entries. This pass is usually offered to people living fifty miles or more from the show and will probably enable the long-distance traveller to get away an hour earlier than the official time of closing.

Any infringement of these rules can be regarded rather seriously. Indeed an exhibitor could be reported to the Kennel Club for, don't forget, the public come to see the entire show—not just part of it. It is well, to note, too, that a dog not actually engaged in the ring, is not supposed to be absent from his bench for more than a quarter of an hour. This ruling is often flouted quite flagrantly, I fear. Nevertheless it is a ruling to ensure that the public shall get value for money and one has to agree that it is a fair and reasonable one. Exhibitors can be reported for non-observance and I am inclined to think there is evidence that show executives are showing signs of tightening up on this regulation.

So now make your way with your dog to your particular ring and await your class at the ringside, on no account allowing your dog to stand inside on a long slack lead. This is annoying and distracting for both judge and stewards, and may quite well upset dogs in the ring. At a crucial moment when every bit of concentration on part of dog and owner is required, far too little attention is paid to this detail. Please do not let your dog be a nuisance in any way to your fellow exhibitors waiting to enter the ring. A bit of a game may seem amusing as two young puppies meet but now is not the time or the place and most exhibitors will be wanting their dogs to settle down and remain trim and groomed looking. In breeds required to look extremely alert exhibitors will occasionally be seen apparently encouraging a dog to get aggressive with some other entry so that their own dog is 'alerted to the full' as ne goes in. This is 'smart alec' stuff, a nuisance to others and

in bad taste. Don't be impressed and think this is clever handling and a good thing to copy. It is infuriating to most people.

The moment arrives and the steward calls your class. This is what you have been waiting for, so make the very most of it. Be business like, be efficient and good luck to you. Go up to the ring steward. Quietly give him the number of your dog as entered in the catalogue and on his bench; he will then check against his catalogue and give you a cardboard disc bearing on it this same number. You must immediately attach this to the lapel of your coat or some other part of your clothing where it can easily be seen by judge, stewards and those spectators at the ringside. Some of these discs have a slot which can be slipped over a coat button. But be prepared with some sort of clip or the good old safety pin and keep this number on every single time you go in the ring with this particular dog until the end of the show. If you are showing more than one dog please do see that you are wearing the right number for the dog you are handling. Don't be vague or careless about this simple procedure. Lots of experienced people, who should know better, err on this point and it is maddening for judge and stewards and can waste precious time. Don't think it is original to wear your card in your hair, on your hat, stuck on your handbag or dangling from the end of the dog's lead, wafting about in the breeze. All of these things I have seen done (mostly by ladies, I do regret to say).

You have now secured your ring number, pinned it on and have been assembled in a rough line all ready to start. A final call may be made for any absentees before noting their non-appearance in the judges' book, and then the steward will usually ask for the dogs to move in single file round the ring until such time as the judge wants to stop them, usually after three or four circuits have been made. While taking this walk round, which is always performed in anticlockwise fashion, your dog should be close to you and always on your left side, that is, the side nearest to the judge; this, of

Opposite: Individual movement is being assessed in the Dalmatian ring whilst the others 'relax'. Remember that many a judge takes a quick look at the 'relaxed' dogs—and often sees something the owner tries to hide when the dog is 'set up'. You have been warned! (Photo: Anne Cumbers)

course, gives the judge a better view of the dog. The reason for this preliminary move is to enable the judge to get an overall first impression of what is in the class and a rough idea of what their movement is like as they pass before him.

If you should be in the lead don't crawl round, but, equally, don't set off as if you were rushing for a train. A brisk easy pace is all that is required of you. In due course, this walk round will be halted at the judge's request, and then will begin the individual examination of each dog in the class. This is the customary procedure: In each ring there will be a table and it is usual for all smallish dogs to be examined by the judge on this table, simply because by doing so the dog is easier to see and, until you have tried to put in a long day of judging, it is hard to imagine what a back-breaking business such examinations can be. In saying smallish dogs, I have in mind dogs of the size of the smaller terriers, Corgis, Basenjis and so on right down, of course, to toy breeds. Bigger breeds, naturally, are judged as they stand on the ground. One by one, the dogs are placed on the table and in the case of a young dog, the owner may be asked the puppy's age, so be ready with the right answer. It is surprising that so many people leave it to this moment to start adding up months and then often have to correct themselves, thus risking irritating the judge.

The judge will then probably want to see the dog's mouth to ensure it is what is required in the particular breed in front of him. Sometimes the judge will make this examination for himself, but quite a number of judges will ask the owner to show him the mouth, and, in the interest of hygiene, this is possibly the best thing to do. Remember that it is the bite that must be inspected so do not hold the dog's mouth wide open as though a judge wished to inspect tonsils—it is the bite which requires inspection, so hold the upper and lower teeth together. The dog may have an edge to edge bite. He may have a scissor bite which, to all intents and purposes, means that the inside of the teeth in the upper jaw will rest close against the outside of the teeth in the lower jaw, lying against each other like the blades of a pair of scissors. Then again he may be undershot as is required in some breeds. This means that the lower jaw is protruding beyond the upper. In the case of the Boxer the teeth in front of the mouth lying between the two large canines in the lower jaw must be in an absolutely straight line whereas the upper jaw must be curved. At the same time the dog is undershot.

Having satisfied himself the judge will go over the dog, looking at his eyes, his expression and ear carriage, his bone, which may be too light in structure or too heavy according to the breed. He will consider the dog's topline, his front, his reach of neck and the balance of his foreface (according to the requirements of his particular breed). Next comes a look at various other points: quality and texture of his coat, his spring of rib, depth of brisket, length, turn of stifle, feet, tail set and other things perhaps peculiar to the breed being judged.

Following the table examination, most judges will require the exhibit to satisfy him in the matter of sound movement. He will usually ask the first one in the class to walk to a certain point and back or he may ask an exhibitor to walk away from him, walk across the top of the ring (so that the dog can be viewed from the side) and return to the judge, describing a triangle. Whatever is required, be quick on the uptake and do what everybody else is doing. In the matter of this simple exercise I find most intelligent people can seem extremely dense and it is surprising how many seem to find it difficult to walk in a straight line. I used to feel that this was a test prescribed at police stations for those who had dined too well, rather than wisely. But I am not so sure about it now. Remember it is not *your* movement but that of the *dog* which is under inspection. So try to walk away from the judge in a straight line keeping the dog beside you on as loose a lead as can be managed. This gives the judge a chance to see whether the dog moves freely and is not cow hocked (which really means that his hocks are not much closer together than his hind feet) or the opposite, bow legged, or as it is called in some breeds, 'hoopy'. At the same time he will notice whether the dog's feet are rightly placed as he moves away and that he doesn't turn his feet out or inwards, both tendencies counting as faults.

If asked to walk the dog across the ring from a sideways view, once again your judge will look for freedom of movement, and what, in the dog world, we call 'thrust'. If a dog has not got thrust in his hind action, he has nothing to propel his body forward and, putting it as plainly as possible, he appears to make a deal of effort

without covering much ground. To have freedom and thrust in the backquarters, he must have plenty of flexibility in hocks and make good use of it. In certain breeds in which angulation is a very big feature such as Alsatians, the view of the angulation in movement from the side is very important indeed. To match the hindquarters it is equally necessary for a dog to be free in his forequarters. A bad shouldered dog will frequently have a constricted stilted sort of action which seems to be putting a brake on the effort from the hindquarters to press forward and cover the ground. As the dog returns to the judge it can be seen whether he turns his feet out and this fault is frequently associated with an undue tightness at the elbow but perhaps the dog turns his feet in as he walks to the judge. Does he toe in, as we term it? This pigeon-toed action is frequently coupled with loose protruding elbows. Does the front of the dog seem straight? That is, do his legs seem equally far apart at his feet as they do across his chest? Does he appear to sprawl or is he bow-legged? Any of these faults can be seen as the dog walks towards one, in a straight line.

There are breeds which have very individual hind movement. The Newfoundland rolls, the Old English Sheepdog paces, the Chow and the Keeshond have very individual movements (which are not alike). However, in general the movement of the legs should appear to be straight from either the hip or the elbow, neither bowing outwards or knocking at the knees, but the faster a dog moves the more likelihood the feet will move closer together in order to keep the body balanced.

Again it must be remembered that although most breeds are required to have straight fronts, especially the terriers, a certain latitude in degrees of straightness are permissible in certain breeds. One thinks of the Cardigan Corgi with a slightly bowed front and, of course, the Bassett Hound with its heavily knuckled front, so individual to this hound. So much then for your dog's exhibition of how to move. The judge will ask you to return to line with your

Opposite: Examining the mouth of a dog should not involve risk to life and limb. Training for this exercise should start at an early age and a gentle opening of the mouth by experienced strangers soon achieves the desired results. (Photo: Anne Cumbers)

rivals in this class and you will remain there until each entry in the class has been 'gone over'.

Most judges will then refresh their memories of the class as a whole and proceed to make their final selections, which they will line up in the centre of the ring all facing the same way. Taking their judging book they will then make the necessary markings while the chief steward calls out the numbers of the winning dogs and hands out those coveted prize cards. Keep your dog showing his best, for a judge sometimes changes his mind at the last minute and it is not over till your number is down in the judging book. Then, if you are lucky enough to be in the first three, keep in your position until the judge has made the notes he requires for his report printed in the dog papers. Accept your award with a 'thank you'.

If you are entered for the following class stand aside and wait until the steward calls the next class into the ring, and then ask him where, as a previous competitor, he would like you to take up your position. It is customary, as judging advances, for all entries which have been examined by the judge in previous classes to be put on one side of the ring in their order of previous judging, while the newcomers are being assessed. When these have been done it may well be that the judge does not think them as good as your dog and you will therefore win this class too. Alternatively, he may find one only which he thinks better than yours, in which case you will be placed second. It may be that you will be required to come into the centre of the ring for the judge to get a view of your dog standing or walking near one of the new dogs for the sake of comparison upon a certain point.

Different judges have somewhat different approaches to the job in hand. Watch the particular methods of the judge and do your best. Unobtrusively fit into the general scheme of things, be ready when required and quick on the uptake to obey the instructions of the steward. By so doing you will be helping both judge and steward to get their job done with as little effort and inconvenience as possible. Take your days up and your days down (and believe me, you'll have them) cheerfully and you will be establishing a sound reputation with your fellow exhibitors. Sometimes, for a variety of reasons, a dog is only entered in one class, and this class he wins. Directly the *open* dog class has been finished, there will be a request for all unbeaten dogs to come into the ring for the awarding of 'best of sex'. Therefore this 'one class' dog, having won his only class, falls into this category and must be kept handy and ready to be back in the ring at the appropriate time to 'challenge' for the top award. At a championship show it could mean a challenge certificate (C.C.) or ticket, as this award gets called, and this is a third of the way to making your dog a champion. So you will keep an eye on general progress and be ready for this great moment, won't you? By the way, if you win any card, be it first or merely 'commended', directly you can, take it and put it over your dog's bench in the place allotted. When you have done this, stand back and look at it. And, if it is your very first award at a dog show it will give you a thrill, something you'll never forget. Let us hope it will be the forerunner of many more.

After the show

Well, win or lose, it is all over and now the rush begins to get out as quickly as possible and strike the trail home—some by car, some by train, some by coach. Here, I venture to think, it is not only the beginner who could learn something of what not to do—so earning gratitude from the dog.

There can be little doubt that a show is not the average dog's idea of bliss; in fact, quite seriously, I think for a great many dogs it presents a long wearing day of noise and turmoil which adds up to a considerable nervous strain. By this I do not for one minute suggest that I am not in favour of shows—of course not—but I think it is a very good plan to make them as bearable as possible for the dog. This is not pure sentimentality—it pays dividends. Sometimes the shy nervous puppy, by careful and sympathetic handling and care, can be got to the stage when, if he doesn't enjoy them at least he accepts them calmly, philosophically if you like. You are much more likely to get a card or two with a dog like this than with the dog who never seems to get over the first hair-raising show which can so easily wreck his chances for ever and a day.

So when it is all over, his job is done but yours may not be. Get your dog out of the show as quietly and as calmly as you possibly can. If you can manage the time, let the first mad rush for the exits

get over and leave quietly. If you have a smallish dog carry him for they so easily get stepped on and terrified. I remember leaving one of the Olympia shows in London and seeing a young Afghan in the crush, get away from his owner, and when I last saw him, looking terrified, he was galloping crazily down the crowded road in between a mass of buses and cars—a sorry sight.

If our exhibitor has taken advantage of one of these long distance coaches organized by some canine society, then at all costs 'don't miss the bus' but do try and let the dog walk around a bit and relieve himself before boarding the coach homewards. Some dogs will go the whole day at a show without attending to these matters, so don't add another four or five hours on a coach to his difficulties, will you? If the journey is to be made by estate car or van then see, once the dog is aboard, that you give him a comfortable bed; and if the weather is bleak and the dog has a short thin coat, wrap him up in a rug. It is so easy in winter, say, for a dog to come out of a heated hall and get into an icy cold car for his homeward journey. Give him a drink of milk and a snack to help him on his way and likely as not he will settle down in the vehicle he knows and travel home very comfortably.

On arrival home see that he has a nice clean kennel or bed to which he can retire in peace. Give him a decent appetizing meal and let him settle down undisturbed—it is quite surprising to me how tired dogs seem to get. I often let them lie in quite late the next morning and they seem glad of it.

Opposite: Sheepskin inside, waterproof outside: ideal protection from the elements is afforded by this coat. (Photo: Anne Cumbers)

6

JUDGES AND JUDGING

It is a great compliment to be invited to judge and many people long for the time when they will be asked to officiate in this capacity. Indeed, some aspiring persons will write to show secretaries and secretaries of breed societies requesting that their names shall be put forward. So many seem to feel that they have claims and could distinguish themselves in this direction. Unhappily, those who push themselves forward sometimes prove to be far less successful than those more humble folks who draw back and need to be persuaded.

Although judging is vastly interesting, judges are criticised so much by unsuccessful exhibitors that at times one wonders why some of them continue to accept judging assignments at all. The positive aspects of the job outweigh the negative, however, and as the years go by one's back becomes fairly broad. I think one also has to resign oneself to the fact that, try as one may, judges and judging are a great talking point for certain exhibitors who, from the ringside, can see untold faults in other people's dogs and feel, at the same time, that their own dogs are perfect. These good souls can only conclude, therefore, that when they do not meet the success they are convinced they merit, there is only one conclusion to be reached—either the judge does not know what he is doing or else something very sinister is going on somewhere. When sufficiently roused these people will resort to the columns of dog journals and carry on their crusade to their heart's content or until the editor decides to call a halt.

Let not our beginner be put off by these opening remarks. It is all part of the game and given a sense of humour (without which you had better seek some other recreation) it can all be rather amusing. Believe me, this is the only right approach. Without the permanent grousers and bad losers the dog game would be without some of its most amusing characters.

The appointment of judges

How do judges actually get their appointments? Now judges can be men or women who have been connected with a certain breed or perhaps breeds for some time and who are placed on their breed club's register of judges. From time to time the secretaries of show societies will write to a breed club secretary inviting suggestions for the appointment of a judge for the particular breed under discussion and from these suggestions a show committee will decide. These judges are usually styled specialist judges and give their services, merely in some cases receiving their expenses in travelling and possibly their subsistence to cover the cost of hotel accommodation.

Of course we have, too, quite a number of professional judges, usually termed in dog circles as professional all-rounders, men and women who receive fees for judging, mostly people with vast experience in dogs and dog shows, some of them being in demand to judge all over the world and, in lots of cases, committed to dates anything up to three years ahead. By and large these judges do a magnificent job of work. I have the pleasure of knowing many of them and have a tremendous admiration for their widespread knowledge and their willingness to teach people who approach them in the right manner. I have enjoyed many conversations with them and usually feel the richer in knowledge of dogs as a result.

In the case of a championship show, the judge is faced with awarding the top honours, challenge certificates. These are the property of the Kennel Club and when a dog has been awarded three under three different judges he becomes a champion. To be partly instrumental in elevating a dog to this position is a considerable responsibility and the Kennel Club have to approve a judge. Should the proposed judge be awarding challenge certificates in a breed for the first time he will usually receive from the Kennel Club a questionnaire which will in due course be considered by the appropriate K.C. committee.

How can winners be losers?

The one thing so very many people seem to overlook in the matter of judges and judging is this: a judge is asked to give his opinions on a certain day at a certain show. His opinion is his particular interpretation of the standard of the breed he is asked to judge. At another show another judge might feel quite differently and place dogs accordingly. This is entirely understandable. If it were not so there would be no point in showing at all and the fascinating game of dog showing would collapse like a pack of cards. The longer one is connected with a breed the more firmly is one convinced that no dog is perfect; always one is searching for the composite dog—this one's head, that one's front, the other one's angulation and so on.

How is it then that a dog can be at the top of his class at one show and, perhaps only third or reserve the following week under another judge? There is nothing very odd about this. First our dog in question may be appearing in stronger competition. He may be showing himself much better on one day than on another. But allowing for the fact that our dog is showing decently and, as is often the case, finds himself up against the same animals, the judge, Mr A., likes the general appearance and balance of our dog considerably, failing him a little on an eye that could be darker and perhaps he could move with greater thrust and freedom. All things considered he is placed First. A week later Mr B. finds his rather light eye very detrimental and (a stickler for movement) he penalizes the dog more heavily than Mr A. for sluggish movement, placing the dog that stood next to our dog last week at the top, moving very freely, nice all round conformation, a darker eye than our dog, being excused for the fact that he could, to be ideal, carry a trifle more width between the ears. And so it goes on and unless you are prepared to accept these differing, but at the same time, expert opinions don't embark upon this game.

Always remember that any show schedule makes it quite clear that the exhibitor is called upon to accept the placings of the judge. This is a condition of entering. It is a great pity that more observation is not given to this point.

Does the best dog always win?

One of the most common questions on the part of members of the public is this: 'When one sees a ring full of "best of breed" winners how is it possible for a judge to arrive at a decision as to which dog is best in show'? It is often difficult, of course, but bear in mind a certain judge or perhaps a couple of judges are invited to give their opinions and it is quite possible that other judges might arrive at an entirely different decision.

As to the dogs themselves, the old saying must be remembered, 'every dog has his day' and fashions come and fashions go. In this big ring, which we are discussing, there may well be dogs which on the day of the show have been adjudged best of breed in a breed which is numerically weak, say a dog which for some reason or other seems to be ignored by the public. The breed is today in the hands of a very few people and if all this is accepted as being correct, it may not take a really outstanding specimen to be best of breed such as they are.

I believe knowledgeable racing people can be heard to say of a Derby winner—'Oh yes, he won the Derby all right in a not very outstanding year when the colts were a very moderate lot'. So it stands to reason that a dog in the best of breed ring, battling for the award of best in show, coming from a popular breed and possibly having had to stand up to a lot of competition in the shape of two or three hundred entries, has more to achieve than the dog which stands at the top of the line in a breed with only a dozen or so rivals. This does not mean to say that the small entry best of breed may not be very outstanding and a magnificent specimen, but it is something to bear in mind when watching the experts in the big rings.

By and large those big rings of competition for best in show present a lovely spectacle for the looker-on, although quite frequently now the group system is introduced and that means that all the dogs appear in their correct groups—that is hound group, gundogs, working, utility, terrier and toy groups—and are judged separately, then the final winners of these groups appear again.

For the final selection, the ultimate winner is taken from these six group winners. These awards are very interesting and excitement runs high as the supporters of the various breeds concerned see their favourites well in the picture for the top award. Every time the judge asks the handler to move the dog, applause will break out from the particular breed's supporters. Commentaries are frequently being given and, in fact it is the high spot of every show, Cruft's in particular.

Judges and the judged

Interesting though it is, judging is an arduous task and exhibitors should appreciate this fact. For myself, I can only say as an exhibitor that whilst I may have at times disagreed with a judge's decisions, I have never felt that any particular favouritism was being shown or any dishonesty was being perpetrated. The beginner, anxious, I hope, to enjoy his dog showing and to be respected by those he meets at shows, would be well advised to steer clear of those who are ever ready to grumble and spread rumours. These people do the fancy no good and our new friends should make it a rule that they will not get involved with them. I can assure them their state will be the more gracious. One should try to win well and, equally, to lose well.

There are one or two things that the beginner should know about in relation to correct procedure. To start with, it is an unwritten rule that the exhibitor does not indulge in conversation with the judge until he has finished judging his classes of the breed in which you are concerned. This does not mean that you have to pass by the judge as you enter the show without a nod of the head or a smile (always providing he is an acquaintance or friend, of course). Some people carry this to an excess and look on the ground or up in the sky until the thing becomes ridiculous. It is a rule to observe sensibly, however, both from your own point of view and from the judge's. If you were to rush up and ask him if his wife had recovered from influenza or whether his son had gone back to school etc. it would of course only be a kindly thought. Nevertheless, it is highly probable that some suspicious soul will be watching from afar and already adding two and two together trying hard to make sixteen of it. As I have already said it is best to keep these tiresome people at a distance, but since, they do exist give them as little as you can to work upon. In the ring be polite at all times to the judge and answer briefly and efficiently any question the judge may ask.

Keep alert, so sparing stewards having to ask you several times to move here or there. All this saves the judge time which with a big entry is perhaps of great help. Endeavour to keep a 'poker face' whether you are having a good day or a bad one. You would be surprised how glum people can look if they don't happen to be doing as well as they think they should. When you receive a card it is only good manners surely to say 'thank you' for the steward's voluntary service, whether it be the first prize or highly commended. Once I remember an enraged exhibitor being handed a 'reserve' when hoping to do better, and promply tearing it up and throwing the pieces in the air.

When it is all over and if you are really thirsting for the judge's opinion on your dog, wait your moment and (accompanied by your dog) politely ask if this opinion could be given. Most judges are very willing to do their best to help the beginner. I say 'accompanied by your dog' for some people have a way of rushing up just as the judge is leaving the ring, having maybe handled a great many dogs from perhaps 10.30 in the morning and it is now five in the afternoon, and saying 'What didn't you like about my puppy in the first class?' This is really aggravating because maybe the puppy was liked quite a lot but others were liked better. It is much more sensible to say, 'Would you be good enough to tell me what you think of this puppy which was shown in one or two classes under you today?'

Having received the expert opinion—and if it differs from your own, accept that opinion with grace—please do not embark upon an argument. You enter the show on the understanding that the judges' opinion is final on the day. If you disagree strongly then remember the remedy lies in your own hands. You need not show under him or her again, need you? But don't arrive at this decision hastily or just because *your* dog has not done well. The judge may well be right!

7

THE LANGUAGE OF THE DOG SHOWS

I have just been looking through the comments written by various judges at a recent championship show and it strikes me that many a beginner could be puzzled by some of the terms used by those with much experience to describe a dog's qualities or faults. It is just the same in the world of cattle, horses and in fact any form of livestock. In this chapter I do not expect to cover by any means all of these forms of expression; in fact, one keeps on hearing things that are new. However, if a number of them are briefly explained the beginner may begin to feel rather more at home.

Front
I have often produced a puppy for an intending purchaser and praised its good front only to find, in a very few minutes, that I was not in the least understood. When this word is used, it is dealing with the construction and consequent appearance of the forelegs in relation to the dog's chest and shoulders. As an example, go and stand face to face with a good Whippet (I choose a Whippet because this breed's fineness of coat and particular height gives us a very good picture). You will note that firstly the elbows lie close to the dog and as the legs proceed to the ground they remain an equal distance apart, so that they appear to leave the dog's body at right angles and stand at right angles to the ground at the point of contact with the foot. Consequently the dog does not seem—to use a human description—to be either bow-legged or knock-kneed.

In almost every breed a straight front is desired, whether the particular breed be a wide dog or a narrow dog when viewed from the forward position. Offhand I can only think of the Cardigan Corgi, Bassett Hound and Peke as notable exceptions to the

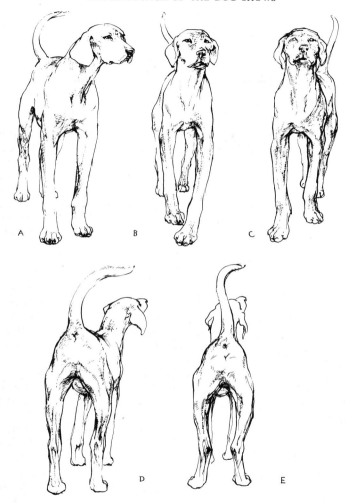

Illustrating: A *correct (straight) front;* B *'pinning';* C *'dishing';* D *correct rear;* 'cow-hocked'.

majority of dogs for which this sort of front is highly desirable. It will be easily appreciated that a dog lacking this quality cannot truly approach you well and freely.

In relation to this matter the expression *tied in elbow* is often used. Just stand with your arms by your side and press the elbows into your sides. What happens? The arm is immediately restricted and the wrist and hands tend to turn out. Likewise the terms *out of elbow, slack at elbow* is just the reverse. Leaving the arms at the sides, turn the elbows out, immediately the hands and wrists turn inwards. So it is with the dog, and no dog with these basic faults will ever walk towards you truly, I find.

Pinning and dishing

Remaining with the same part of the dog's anatomy, if the front is good, the feet are required to point straight ahead, but sometimes an otherwise passable front will be completely spoilt by one or both feet turning inwards or outwards. And when this is evident, the dog often tends to walk on one side of the foot only. When the feet turn in (although this may be partly due to front) as he approaches, we talk about the dog *pinning*. Curiously, quite a few gun dogs have this tendency I notice. In reverse, if the feet seem to turn out we refer to *dishing*, though this sometimes covers the dog which appears to scoop or flick the lower part of the foreleg outwards when it is bent in moving forward. This is quite a common thing to see in horses. When the feet seem to cross as they walk *plaiting* is the word.

Loose in the foot or *splay footed* pretty well speaks for itself, I think, for this indicates a foot with widely separated toes and a flat soft look about it, usually resulting from lack of exercise, which can be accompanied by nails which are too long. Sometimes a judge will write that *a dog leaves you well*, and in this case it means that the animal appears to move away soundly and freely, showing no signs of being *cow-hocked*, which describes hind legs which converge at the hock. In bad cases the hocks almost knocking together (if the hind legs are very close the dog will probably *brush*). The opposite of this is sometimes called *hoopy*, in other words, bow-legged.

Terms for movement

When a sound dog moves away from the viewer the legs should remain at the same distance away from each other from the body down to the feet and one should just see the hind pads as he moves away (the dog *goes wide* when his hind feet appear too far apart as he travels away).

Plenty of *thrust* is a common term meaning that the dog steps out in the front and there is plenty of *forward propulsion* in the hind legs to drive the animal ahead as he moves when viewed from the side. Now to do this, the dog must have a sufficiency (within his breed) of *angulation* at the *hock*. In a very straight-hocked dog there will not be enough spring to give the dog anything but a very jerky stilted appearance as he moves. Have a look at an Alsatian or German Shepherd as some prefer to call him. He is probably the one to convey a really good example of angulation. Movement or *gaiting*, as Alsatian breeders term it, is of great importance in this breed and it is interesting to study the tremendous sweep of the

Angulation of the hind leg in the Alsatian or German Shepherd.

hind leg from the body down to well angulated hock, which should be reasonably low to the ground to complete the desired picture.

Observe that in any breed requiring capability of speed there is a great distance between what we may call the hip or the haunch bone and the point of hock. Only if a dog is built on these lines can it have the agility desired, such agility emanating from the hindquarters as in a steeplechaser or show jumper. Afghans, Salukis, Borzois, Greyhounds and Deerhounds as well as Alsatians all possess this very individual quality but they all have to be very speedy dogs, capable of tremendous acceleration when required.

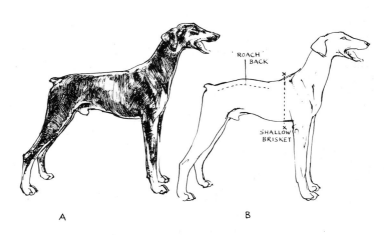

Illustrating: A *straight back and depth of brisket;* B *'roached' back and shallow brisket.*

Brisket

Judges often refer to *greater depth of brisket necessary* or *wants to let down to elbow.* Especially in young immature dogs viewed from the side, the *brisket* or *chest* seems to finish an inch or so above the point where the elbow joins up with the body and it presents a rather weak unpleasing line. As the animal develops and puts on weight, the picture improves in the case of a young dog still in the growing, or perhaps one should say 'filling out', stage.

Head to tail terms

Dogs are described as being *reachy*, excelling or lacking in reach, when referring to the neck, that is from the point of shoulder to the head. Breeds vary considerably but *within* its breed, a dog must have *sufficiency of neck line*. Complete lack of it gives a dog what we call a *stuffy* appearance. *Long cast* or *long in the coupling* means that the animal is too *long* to balance with the rest of its conformation, and, of course the reverse. However, I would say that the former is a far more common complaint. Perhaps it is that so many breeds seem to require a short back as part of their standard.

When the position of the tail calls for comment one perhaps reads *too low, set on*, which refers to the position of the root of the tail. A low *set on* will give a sloping look to the *croup* or *hindquarters* which in some breeds is undesirable, while a too high *set on* will spoil the top line of certain breeds requiring a graceful sweeping line over the *croup* or rump of the dog. This especially applies to breeds which naturally carry long tails low (Collies, Alsatians for instance).

Roaching describes the exhibit that seems to have a humpy back. A great deal of attention is paid to the *top line* and while some dogs naturally have this tendency, other dogs can give this impression by the very way they stand in the ring. Unwillingness to show by dogs that are shy, or cold weather at an open show can perhaps be contributing factors. When a dog is described as *a trifle strong headed* a judge usually finds the exhibit somewhat coarse and lacking in the refinement he expects to find in the breed. *Rise of skull* refers to the height and angle at which, let us call it, the *brow* or *forehead* of the dog rises from the *stop* which in humans would be called the bridge of the nose.

Other terms

Well up to size implies that a dog is plenty big enough and were he any bigger he would be too big. *Furnishings* refer to breeds which have fringes on their legs, ears and on their tail. Sometimes a judge will write *lacking the furnishings required* which usually implies that the dog is partly *out of coat* or in the process of changing his coat.

Spring of rib seems to speak for itself. All dogs, within their breed limits, must have well developed spring of rib to give them *heart room*. Obviously the general contour of, say, a Greyhound is vastly different from a Mastiff; both should be powerful, though one is built on massive lines and the other on very muscular but slender lines, but no breed of dog should lack *spring* or he will look *slab sided* which is really the same as describing a man as being flat chested.

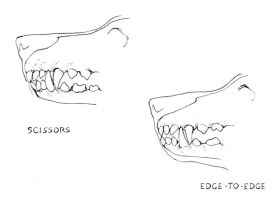

SCISSORS

EDGE-TO-EDGE

The scissors bite and edge-to-edge bite.

Outlook is a description which appeals to me. It really is the right word, applicable especially to Afghans, Salukis and Deerhounds. Stand in front of a good Afghan. He seems to look right through one right out into the distance and that's how it should be.

All these terms and many others will become customary to the newcomer to shows as time goes by. Other terms are rather restricted to certain breeds. For instance in Poodles one talks about *leathers* (not ears). This will apply to most hounds too, and when discussing the latter breeds you will find that *sterns* not tails are the order of the day. Again, in some breeds the word *plume* is preferred to tail. Finally, mouths in most breeds come in for criticism. Sometimes one will hear of an *edge to edge bite* which describes itself, or a *scissor bite* acceptable in so many breeds in which the front teeth of the upper jaw just cover those in the lower jaw, like the blades of a pair of scissors. Some breeds are naturally *under-shot* and perhaps the most individual is the Boxer.

So much then for some of the jargon of the dog show. It will be found worthwhile to get accustomed to it all. The reading of judges' reports becomes so much more interesting if you know what the other fellow is talking (or writing) about.

8

COUNTING THE COST

Before the inflationary period which began to hit the dog shows in 1975, it was possible for a limited number of exhibitors to make a small profit on showing their dogs, but these days are now gone. The price of petrol and the necessary increase in the entry fees, and in some instances, the lack of any prize money at all, has resulted in the hobby becoming quite expensive if it is hoped to attend the many championship shows held all over the country.

Do breeders make profits?

Perhaps there are some who make a profit from breeding puppies, but these are usually the undesirable 'puppy farmers'. The average exhibitor is lucky if the sale of puppies even covers the vet's bill, their feeding, the stud fee, and part of the outlay in going to the shows in an effort to prove the quality of the stock they produce. Many people regard it as a hobby or pastime from which they get a lot of fun and make a lot of friends with similar interests. The latter are, perhaps, the backbone of the dog game and one will find these same people absolutely thrilled when they have the occasional spectacular sale to help balance up some of their expenditure.

Here again the man in the street will sometimes say that this or that person makes a lot of money out of dogs. A well-known theatre producer once told me that he was surprised to hear I was still interested in pursuing my career in the theatre as he knew I lived in the country and bred dogs. This I found particularly hard since I am afraid that my wife and myself could be described as being particularly uncommercial in this field. We seldom advertise, never send puppies away to complete strangers and scarcely ever part with mature dogs. I am afraid our own dogs become our friends, perhaps nearly our relations, with all their individual faults and virtues. They and their ancestors have given us a lot of fun and pleasure.

It is said, however, that the 'looker on' sees most of the game and since I have so many friends in dogs, have served for many years on breed club committees and have been judging for nearly twenty-five years, I feel I have collected quite a deal of information on the subject of finance and dogs.

Breeders' problems

It is the easiest thing in the world to collect a large stock of dogs. The owner of, say, three bitches, can, if they happen to whelp about the same time, soon find he is faced with fifteen or twenty mouths to feed. But can you sell them all just when you think you can? A friend in the Alsatian world once had occasion to go, in the course of dog business, to a small house about the size of the average council house. Imagine her surprise when she saw peering from various windows no less than fourteen Alsatians' heads. Another woman I came across with a quite small back garden had thirtytwo Boxer puppies running around in it. She was not well-known in the breed and had had no enquiries for her puppies. Yet another person, again not well-known in his breed, had seventeen Borzoi puppies in a yard adjoining his house. This sort of haphazard production is really no good to anyone. Sooner or later the overstocked owner gets frantic as his food bills mount and inoculation bills come in, and in desperation he cuts his prices to ridiculously low figures in order to dispose of some at least of his stock. This is no good for the owner, no good for his fellow breeders and probably no good for the dogs themselves.

The big breeder, too, has many problems. A big kennel means big food bills, a kennelmaid or some sort of help, constant showing with all its attendant expenses, and constant advertising as well. For here decisions as to the quality of puppies must be made at a pretty early stage or kennels get filled which are required for other litters coming along. Further it is a fact that prices do not increase in proportion to expenses as young stock grow on. Dog puppies probably present the bigger problem for it is a fact that far more people today are well informed about the keeping of bitches and indeed many more people these days seem to prefer them as pets.

There is not much future in the serious exhibitor's kennel for anything other than really top grade dogs. The rest do not really get anywhere in the show ring and in consequence are not in demand as stud dogs. Therefore this type of dog is far better fixed up in a pet home as soon as his potentialities can be assessed. What may be termed, from a show point of view, a second rate bitch, if she has no very glaring faults but carries useful blood lines and is soundly constructed, may prove a very good brood bitch and be capable of continually producing show-quality puppies capable of achieving in the ring what she herself cannot do. I am of the opinion that this type of puppy is far easier to place when it comes to selling.

Undoubtedly a really good stud dog is a very rewarding addition to any kennel, but he must have a good record in the show ring and for this reason breeders work so hard and travel so far, yes, and spend so much, trying to get the dog his qualifying certificates and thereby make him a champion. It's a curious fact that in many cases the third and last 'ticket' required to achieve championship status seems by some strange quirk to be a difficult one to get, and I have known dogs taken from one end of the country to the other in search of this and always seemingly being just beaten to the post. All this can be very expensive since a dog of this position usually is only eligible for one class, that is *Open Dog* and if he wins this his reward would be two pounds at the most, which doesn't help very much when, on top of entries, the cost of long journeys has to be taken into account. I had a friend in a certain big breed who had to fight hard to make her dog into a champion (*make him up* is the usual showgoer's term) and she informed me that she thought it must have cost her some three hundred pounds to do it. I felt she deserved some substantial stud fees after all that effort. It must be remembered also that it is more often than not your potential stud dog which is the one most likely to attract large offers from overseas buyers.

Breeding as a business

Of course, big kennels, as business concerns, can make claims for all sorts of expenses—labour in the kennels, food bills, transport to shows and expenses attending them, vet's bills, telephones, correspondence, advertising, etc. but accounts will have to be carefully recorded and presented and the authorities will require to satisfy themselves that the whole thing is a genuine business undertaking.

Human beings being what they are, there are many many people always determined to maintain that they make money regardless of what the other chap does. I think they are not very numerous, especially if their own labour is to be charged at a proper rate. A spectacular price must be very pleasant to receive (personally I've never had one) but let us say a thousand pounds for an export sale is not a thousand a year or anything like it. There are so many 'near misses' in the dog world that leave their kennels for the mere £25–£30 (the travelling costs to a championship show in Scotland from the south of England) and depart, we hope, to a nice kind home. These are the dogs that play 'ducks and drakes' with the finance department.

It is a strange and maddening fact too, that one seldom seems to have what is required. If one has lots of dog puppies, then bitches are required and vice versa. So often one has the wrong colour or the wrong sex, and I suppose all of us know the wrong type of purchaser—the man, woman or tiresome child who, within a matter of minutes, makes us who love our dogs feel 'oh no, not at any price'.

Conclusion

My readers may feel, as they come to the end of this chapter, a sense of disappointment, a feeling that I have been discouraging. Not really; don't be put off. Go into this thing with your eyes open and I expect you'll feel like most of us that all the trials and tribulations are worth it in the long run.

9

OR SO IT SEEMS TO ME

Many happy years in the dog game have provided me with certain observations which I pass on to my beginner friends for what they may be worth, to be accepted or otherwise, as the reader may be disposed.

Breeding bores

If you really want to enjoy life in the dog show world avoid at all costs getting involved in what appears to be a mischief-making clique—certain types give the impression of extracting a deal of excitement and fun out of imagining all sorts of shady goings-on. Half the rumours involved are either unfounded or grossly exaggerated, and the other half are quite impossible to even begin to prove. To get involved in this sort of thing only makes for bad friends and, in time, show going can become an embarrassment instead of a pleasure.

Don't become a disciple of the sort of exhibitor who from the ringside can see every possible fault in other people's dogs and other people's judging, for that is the quick way to become one of the crashing bores which exist in most breeds. I am afraid that some people do not seem able to differentiate between healthy keenness, which is good, and letting themselves develop a tiresome intensity. I was amused to learn that a very well-known judge had a good way of dealing with any lady thoroughly worked up because her dog had had 'a day down' and was only waiting to get hold of the judge to grouse or argue about his placings. He used to get in the first shop by opening the conversation with the words 'Now relax, dear lady!' a rather defeating beginning.

Then again, I think it is well to remember that whilst there are an enormous number of people very interested in dogs, and indeed very fond of them, nevertheless there are many more who could not care less about what won the puppy class at such and such a show! Neither do a lot of people want to hear all about your latest 'whelping' with every detail. I would be most interested and doubtless so would many others 'in dogs' but the rest will find it rather 'off putting'.

Don't lose your wife (or husband)

I knew a certain lady, very immersed in dogs, who spent the night with some friends of mine and only one person in the family went in for dogs. She spent the whole evening and kept her hosts up till about 2 a.m. indulging in a non-stop graphic lecture about the mating and whelping of her bitches. So boring for those who do not happen to be interested. This is a disservice to the world of dogs and extremely boring to others. There's plenty of opportunity to get this off one's chest at the various shows we attend. It is very useful to have the odd members of one's family sufficiently interested to lend a hand occasionally, do a bit of exercising or help feed some puppies, etc. This is a piece of good fortune to treasure and encourage so don't run the risk of losing this interest by pouring all your dog show disappointments too heavily on the family or you may find yourself in sole residence.

I talked to an extremely nice woman recently who surprised me by saying she had more or less given up dogs. On being asked why, she informed me that she had found a new hobby—her husband. In the conversation that followed she told me that she had suddenly realized that she had let herself become so heavily involved in dogs that she could never go anywhere, do anything, take any holidays, because she always seemed to be tied at home with bitches whelping, tiny puppies, etc. All through these years her husband had patiently put up with these difficulties and now she thought that he should come first. A praiseworthy decision, or so it seems to me.

It is so easy to get to the 'too many but not enough' stage. Too many to care for without the job being a time-taking labour, not enough to justify any paid help in the way of a kennelmaid. A large number of people get into this difficult position and however much we like our dogs it's not the best way to get full enjoyment out of them, so remember, forewarned is forearmed.

I once heard of a husband whose long-suffering wife decided she must 'walk out'—she just could not take seven Afghans in her small suburban kitchen. I can see her point, can't you? I had a friend, married to a nice but not particularly dog-minded husband. He just, with all the will in the world, could not put up with two Irish Wolfhounds sleeping in the bedroom.

An American President coined a most useful word, 'normalcy', and I think we dog fanciers must cling to this with all our might, or so it seems to me.

Shows and ourselves

I have often thought we could all help to make dog shows a bit more attractive to the general public. I know it can be argued that the people come to see the dogs but nevertheless the presentation of the main attraction does count for something I feel. At Crufts and at the Richmond Show—both held at Olympia, one in February and the other in December—we can find the rings looking spotless under the lights and devoted to the really spectacular parts of the shows. But elsewhere there is often a lot to be desired in the matter of something really arresting for the public to see. At the big Westminster Show at Madison Garden, New York, the high spots of the show come along in the evening with judges in dinner jackets, big spotlights on the rings, television cameras, commentaries and all the presentation of a big event. It must be admitted, the spectacle is quite an exciting one, building up as it does to the supreme awards.

I hope some day that someone will be enterprising enough to try something of the sort here. I rather think that exhibitors themselves are inclined to be short-sighted over this. As things appear at present, the average exhibitor could not care less about the man in the street who pays his money at the turnstile and brings his family to see the dogs. But here perhaps are many potential buyers of pet puppies. Here perhaps are the breeders and fanciers of the future. If everyone does whatever may be in his power to help make the members of the paying public enjoy themselves to the full and feel that they have been not only amused but instructed as well, then I think the public paying good money at the gates would be much bigger than it is.

And this thought leads us to ourselves. Do we try to present our dogs as immaculately as possible—do we even try to make ourselves look as reasonably worthy of our good looking dogs as is possible? I don't think we do. We mere males in the dog game seem to succeed in looking drearily inconspicuous, which is probably as it should be, fairly informal country-type attire seems to be pretty much the order of the day. But what about the ladies? We are not holding a fashion parade and we are well aware that the good judge is not looking at 'the other end of the lead', but surely in many cases improvements could be made, and a fairly smart workmanlike attire be produced. It is not given to many women to be 'Miss Worlds' and indeed it is given to fewer men to look right for super-men body beautiful contests, but I sometimes wish a film could be made of some of the clothes worn by some of the ladies in some of the positions they find it necessary to adopt in the ring. The impact would not fail to be considerable and some new ideas would surely be forthcoming.

Mink coats and stiletto shoes are not the things to lap around the ring gaiting your Alsatian, but there is, of course, a happy medium. I can, of course, think of many people who strike just the right note. The efficient little lady who shows a big breed in smart looking slacks and a suede sheepskin short coat. This, with a trim 'hair do' looks workmanlike, attractive and dead right. I can also think of the lady showing a smart little Mexican Chihuahua, who was simply, suitably, but elegantly attired with a delightful Mexican Sombrero, that simply shouted 'Paris'.

Well, we can't all look 'with it', to quote what I am informed is 'The beat' language. But at least we can do our best to look reasonably suitable for the occasion, don't you agree?

10

FLESH AND BLOOD

I am well aware as I write this chapter that I am 'sticking my neck out'. I am well aware that most, if not all, of my readers will exclaim, 'Well, this does not apply to me in any way. I should never be like this or ever become like this'. If this assertion is correct, then I am delighted to hear it. Also, I am aware of the fact that, should any of the hardened exhibitors ever honour me by reading these few lines, then I will be accused of exaggeration or an excess of sentimentality, by perhaps a few of them—those who either do not want to face up to facts or those who just do not care.

However, the more I have had to do with animals the more surprised I am to notice that there are so many people who do not seem to remember that we are dealing with flesh and blood. I am afraid the dog world is not free of these people either.

Need it all be quite so hard-headed and commercialized? I wonder. One knows that the person in livestock for a bread and butter job (and a hard enough way of life it is) will tell you that it is uneconomical to let stock grow old on your hands, there is no room for your unproductive stud dog, not in much demand—he must go. Your elderly brood bitch must be disposed of while she can still be used as a puppy factory by somebody, and can therefore have a sales-value. Your pet puppies must be got rid of at all costs and if they end up with a dealer or in a pet shop well it's just too bad or so what? These are probably the people who will put a puppy on the train without any idea of what sort of home awaits it. This is the sort of person who will tell you that they are in the game to suceed so they cannot carry passengers.

Never having been particularly commercial about our dogs, my wife and I have always felt that we would willingly sacrifice a few prize cards in return for a certain peace of mind about our dogs. From our point of view, it has paid dividends, for when Christmas comes round we get numbers of cards from owners of our families of puppies—in fact sometimes they create quite a problem as we try to figure out exactly which lot of puppies contained the old dog in the picture—but we like it that way. I started out to be a farmer, and in dealing with horses, cattle and, in fact any form of livestock, I have never felt that one lost anything by remembering that a firm but gentle and understanding approach was the way to get the worthwhile results in the long run. It is a pity that so many people allow themselves to get so over keen about it all.

Dogs can be maddening, especially those that are so lively at home and go do down like pricked ballons in the ring. But it is seldom a matter of unwillingness to please, it is more often than not plain stage fright, a feeling of frustration and unhappiness at the noise, the bustle and all the strange people milling around. But how much is it your fault? Have you put enough time into exercising the dog where he can see the strange sights to be seen (and there are plenty to be seen at dog shows too)? Have you had so many dogs on your hands that he's been put into exercise runs because you just haven't had time? Has he been bundled into a box or car in the early hours with no chance of a few minutes to attend to the calls of nature? Before you blame the dog, be like a good show jumper and say first 'Did I do anything wrong!' Remember that a long day at a show and perhaps a long journey, can exhaust a dog's nervous system. So see that he travels home to a worthwhile meal and a warm bed (whether he's won or not, doesn't matter).

I remember once seeing what was a pitiful sight outside Olympia, after a big show. I had remained talking to friends and the great hall was nearly empty. As I made my way to the station which almost adjoins, I stood on the bridge and watched an elderly lady exhibitor bound for home with about for smallish dogs on leads. Whether she had been celebrating her successes or drowning her sorrows, I do not know, but I did know she was swaying about and the unhappy little dogs looked miserable and insecure and I wondered what sort of attention they'd get when they did reach home.

It looks very professional for some of our terrier friends to carry their dogs about with one hand under the jaw and the other grasping the dog by the tail. I know he's just been chalked and is ready for the judge, but you are not taking last week's washing to the laundrette—you are handling a living thing and is it necessary? I wonder.

I remember hearing of the case of the small frightened terrier, forgotten and left in the show hall, discovered by the bench dismantling people in the early morning following the show. Perhaps at the risk of annoying some caterers, one might say that some people could be better employed attending to their dogs than the next round of drinks at the bar.

I had the honour of being on the committee of one of the big summer show organisations with a big car park. Oh, the trouble in persuading people not to leave dogs which were not concerned in the show, in shut-up cars on blazing hot days. How many times did the request go out on the loudspeakers. It was not until the very able secretary had a staff of people going around the cars, with the threat that any dogs distressed would be forcibly removed, that some senseless and thoughtless people thought of the inconvenience of repairing a car window and felt compelled to do something about the creatures of flesh and blood inside.

Judges have some place in this chapter too. It's no great demonstration of efficiency to handle small dogs roughly. What must a small dog of four pounds feel like when grabbed by a twelve stone judge and roughly handled? I saw someone judging a toy breed one day and they were being handled as if they were haddocks on a fishmonger's slab. Does this impress you? It doesn't me.

Fortunately the majority of people one meets at shows are not like this at all and set tremendous store by their dogs. Equally they would be the first to agree with this perhaps somewhat depressing chapter. All I ask my reader is this. However keen you may become on this 'game', however absorbed by your successes you may be, please as one old hand to a beginner: 'Remember you're dealing with flesh and blood'.

IF

*(As it might have been written
had Rudyard Kipling been a Dog Fancier)*

by Sherman R. Hoyt

If you can show your dog when all about you
    Are showing theirs and winning every blue;
If you can trust your choice when judges doubt you
    But make allowance for their doubting too;
If you can breed and keep on showing puppies
    To see them given nothing but the gate;
And still keep right on trying to do better
    Unblinded by despair, or rage, or hate.

If you can bear to see the hints you've spoken
    In judges' ears deliberately ignored;
Or see the plans you worked so long on broken
    When stewards write the placings on the board;
If you can hear the ringside gossips yacking
    Of dog show dirt and all that kinda stuff;
And realize, though in truth they're largely lacking,
    You should give heed—not much but just enough.

If you can swear by everything that's holy
    To shut your trap and not help start a row;
You'll be a man the equal of George Foley,
    And if that ain't high praise I don't know how!
If you can do all this and still keep showing,
    No matter what the 'fancy' has to say,
You'll be a dog fanatic most worth knowing,
    And maybe run the AKC some day!

Reproduced by kind permission of POPULAR
DOGS. *Philadelphia, U.S.A., whose courtesy
is gratefully acknowledged.*

INDEX